Praise For Author

"Hi Ian. Well, he says that he knew every answer! Typed 3 pages in fact. How good is that! He is very happy and confident and we are over the moon! Thank you so much for all your time and patience. We did it, we all did it!

Kind regards, from the ecstatic Pope family!"

"Dear Ian. This is a wonderful achievement for him in any circumstances, but especially given his very limited capacity to embrace the demands of VCE English and study in general. Just for him to have sat the exam was an amazing achievement for you both. I believe a study score of 20 is something to be very proud of. Scores are relative to individual circumstances and his situation is most unique. Congratulations to you both!!"

Ros Pretlove, 'Director, WISA Wellbeing in Schools Australia' and 'former Deputy Principal and Head of Wellbeing'

"I think your programs are great for the child's confidence. It works very well because it starts with the basics and builds from there. James has improved in his concentration and ability to get information for his projects."

Jodie, mother of Year 7 student

"We have been thrilled with the work you have done with Suzie over the last year. Thank you for your help and patience with her when she was trying to cope with the school 'issues'. Getting the times tables down pat has made school life much easier for Suzie."

Sally, mother of Grade 5 student

"We love your tutoring program best because you mix it up so nicely with a little bit of everything. Albert's writing has definitely improved."

Bernadette, mother of Grade 1 boy

"He can work out the value of money now and is able to add things in his head where he couldn't before. Ian has done wonders in the weeks he has been teaching Robbie."

Taylor, mother of Year 9 boy

Comments from students at the Year 11 Youth Leadership Workshop at Moama Anglican Grammar School:

"My favourite part was probably the importance of what we had to say. We've done other workshops that were about what others had to say. But today was really about our opinions and how we felt and what we felt we could do better."

"It was funny and engaging but we still learnt a lot. Being able to hear what other people find hard was good and learning new skills that I can use to lead others."

"I enjoyed all of the different aspects that were discussed such as individual, group and around the world leadership. I also enjoyed the short movie clips."

"I enjoyed how relaxed it was and how open we could be. It was fun and we laughed a lot. I have gained the 'secrets' of public speaking and how to approach new people and how to talk to them"

"I enjoyed all aspects and the fact that we could contribute. It was learning in a safe and supportive environment. You were fantastic."

"The comparison of videos of the different types of speeches was good."

"Hearing everyone's opinions about leadership and learning and how I can impart my knowledge and previous experience to others."

Dynamic Teaching

In the 21st Century

GLOBAL
PUBLISHING
G R O U P

Global Publishing Group
Australia • New Zealand • Singapore • America • London

Dynamic Teaching

In the 21st Century

Empowering tools and
strategies for teachers who
want to make a difference

IAN DAVIES

First Edition 2015

National Library of Australia
Cataloguing-in-Publication entry:

Creator: Davies, Ian P. (Ian Phillip), 1954- author

Dynamic Teaching in the 21St Century : Empowering Tools and Strategies for Teachers Who Want to Make a Difference / Ian Davies.

1st ed.
ISBN: 9781925288056 (paperback)

Effective teaching.
Teacher effectiveness.
Educational technology.
Academic achievement.

Dewey Number: 371.102

Published by Global Publishing Group
PO Box 517 Mt Evelyn, Victoria 3796 Australia
Email info@GlobalPublishingGroup.com.au

For further information about orders:
Phone: +61 3 9739 4686 or Fax +61 3 8648 6871

This book is dedicated to my grandchildren and those that may come after them.

May your education be fulfilling, energetic and meaningful and support your individuality, creativity and holistic wellbeing.

IAN DAVIES

Acknowledgements

Writing a book of this nature has been an entirely new experience for me. I had so many ideas, issues, problems and solutions I wanted to talk about, that I found it difficult to put them all into some sort of structure which would create a book that might prove a valuable asset to teachers. So I want to acknowledge a number of people who helped to keep me on track.

To my coach, Debra Woods from Life Fulfillment Coaching, thank you for your supreme coaching skills, your undying belief in me and your words of wisdom that seemed to give me the clarity to finally put pen to paper and express my thoughts in some sort of coherent manner. You have gone beyond the call of duty many times for me Debra. You have my heartfelt thanks and gratitude.

To Darren Stephens and the team at Global Publishing Group, thank you for inviting me into your 2015 How To Write A Best Seller group. Thank you also for your unending support and guidance to bring my book to fruition. To the other authors in the How To Write A Best Seller group, thank you for your input and ideas for my book, your friendship and your support.

To my wife Robyn, who spent many a lonely night watching TV on her own while I typed merrily away on my desktop, a huge thank you. One of your greatest gifts to me is to give me the freedom to follow through on all my wild ideas - like writing a book on education!

To my only daughter, Morgan, thank you. You and Morgi Mac Design were there right from the start for Aussie Kids Coach. Your creative input with design work and product layout for many of my products has been invaluable, and your design work for this book has added to its message and impact.

To my son Corey, thank you. You have been an integral part of this book. I greatly appreciate your proof reading skills and all the feedback you have given me about structure, organisation and clarity.

To my daughter in law, Claire, thank you. Your help with proofing my book and helping me develop the associated products has been invaluable.

To the parents who entrusted the educational wellbeing of their children to me, thank you. It has been a wonderful journey for me to tutor each and every child. But a special thank you to Terry Phillips. He was the one who issued me with the initial tutoring challenge and got me started at tutoring after 20 years of being away from teaching. Your faith in me as William's tutor was critical in those early years as I was often torn with self doubt. This book is the result of the seed you sowed in me.

To the school principals who invited me into their schools to work with a diverse range of students, thank you. Without your support I would never have gained such an intimate insight into the current education system and how it affects the students of today.

And finally to the kids I have worked with, you are the real heroes in this story. To each and every one of you, I give thanks to you for what you have taught me, and for gifting me your authority to teach and coach you.

Contents

Contents

Foreword

If you are a teacher who seeks to work more effectively with young people, you will **want** to read Ian Davies' book, *Dynamic Teaching*. If you are a pre-service teacher – **trust me, you need to read it.** Ian's enthusiasm to share what he has come to understand through decades of work at the coalface of education will guide many people to better practices in schools. Parents/carers and coaches of young people will also gain much from Ian's very accessible story about how to encourage, support and expand possibilities for young people.

I am officially 'green with envy' and immensely relieved at the same time. Many of the ideas and beliefs shared by educators I hold in high regard are presented here. Sage advice about how to teach more authentically and better engage young people in learning has actually found its way into cohesive print, courtesy of an experienced, passionate and caring educator. Ian presents a realistic picture of the challenges we currently face as educators. Better still, he outlines logical ways to overcome those challenges.

The privilege of collaborating with Ian in a school setting was something I experienced for three rewarding years. Working as a deputy principal (Head of Wellbeing) in a secondary school, I was constantly seeking ways to better support our vulnerable students. I heard from a youth worker about Ian, who was successfully tutoring some struggling students in a nearby town. Not only a pragmatic farmer and experienced former primary teacher, Ian is also a qualified life coach. It was a 'red-letter' day when he agreed to work at our school part time, something that has continued for years now, even though I've since moved on.

Ian is a wonderful mentor, coach, tutor, teacher and supporter of students with all manner of personal difficulties, traumatic backgrounds, disability and/or disengagement. He role models a calm, gentle demeanor, along with passion for education and for life. Ian applies persistence, patience, impeccable preparation and thorough follow up in the work he does with young people. In other words, Ian doesn't just 'talk the talk' – he 'walks the walk'. That fact alone makes this book about problems witnessed in classrooms, along with recommended approaches and strategies, so very authentic, valid and worthwhile. In addition, Ian backs up his beliefs with inspirational quotes, relevant statistics and reference to some of the finest practitioners and experts in education. Clearly, Ian has done his homework!

During our collaboration in a school setting, Ian's approaches had measurable impact on our most vulnerable students. For example, a student severely challenged with Autism confidently completed a VCE English exam; traumatized young people learnt how to find meaning in their lives; struggling and/or depressed Koorie students were encouraged to flourish or perhaps just hang in there – stay connected. Many disaffected, disengaged young folk were able to reconnect with learning through Ian's help and belief in them. Working one on one, in small groups and in classroom settings over many years, Ian gained unique perspectives about what does and doesn't work, what engages and disengages, what empowers and sadly, what disempowers.

In his introduction, Ian mentions being galvanized by the birth of his grandsons to write this story and share his wisdom. Like Ian, I've recently experienced the absolute joy of grandchildren arriving in my life. Like Ian, I'm driven to want the world to be a better place for them; for schools to be much more functional; for everyone's children and grandchildren to feel enthusiasm for learning; to experience success and to embrace mistakes and failure as rich learning opportunities. We should all want children to develop endless possibilities for the future and gather valuable life skills during their time in our education system.

Like Ian, I have despaired that our current education system, despite the best efforts of many dedicated and hard working teachers and leaders, is failing too many of our young people. Like Ian, I am passionate about working to

stimulate change to current practices in schools that alienate or stifle students when education should enliven them. Young people should be thriving because of their schooling experiences, not despite them! Education is a privilege that deserves better outcomes in today's fast paced world. We need to learn from the error of our ways, adopt a positive mindset about what will work more effectively in schools then make it happen: teacher-by-teacher, student-by-student, class-by-class, school-by-school, parent-by-parent.

Ian's strong messages about the value of a positive mindset, of meaningful partnerships with parents/carers, careful preparation, sound reflection and the importance of self-science alongside a strong commitment to the 'hidden' curriculum should be embraced by all educational practitioners. He echoes what we seek to achieve with the recent establishment of WISA (Wellbeing in Schools Australia). Ian's reflections on the impact of digital technology in the fields of teaching and learning are also very pertinent. He inspires hope that we can better utilize e-tools for learning and thus minimise the problems currently being experienced by many teachers.

The Australian Federal Government recently completed an inquiry into teacher training and reforms are being sought at university level to better deliver 'classroom-ready' teachers into the workforce. As someone who mentors pre-service teachers for universities, I am driven to want each education graduate around Australia to step confidently into the world of teaching, properly equipped with the approaches and knowledge they need to best support each and every student in their care. I know they still have much to learn and in too many instances they will learn the hard way, or not at all.

Commencing employment as a teacher is a giant leap that can be more traumatic than fulfilling for some. The current dropout rate occurring amongst graduate teachers is appalling. Many have been overwhelmed by their transition to the educational workforce, yet schools need these graduate teachers to thrive. If pre-service and registered teachers alike read *Dynamic Teaching* and absorb

Ian's wisdom, their chances of achieving success in one of the most worthwhile careers that exist – teaching – will be considerably boosted. Like Ian, they will understand the importance of operating above the magic line.

Thank you, Ian for your wonderful contribution to education.

Ros Pretlove
Director
WISA Wellbeing in Schools Australasia Pacific

An Introduction To 21st Century Teaching

Miss Cassie Young is teaching a Year 9 maths class at the moment. It is the final period of the day and despite Miss Young's diligent preparation and passion for teaching, things are not going well for her Year 9 group. The topic the class are working on is Algebra and in spite of Miss Young's best efforts to explain how to expand (x + 3) (x - 5) there are a handful of kids who just don't get it and another handful who won't even try to get it.

An attempt to show the class a video tutorial on Algebra has failed due to an issue with the equipment and as the class is asked to settle down to work on Questions 1, 2, 4 and 6 from Chapter 3.2 in their text book, Miss Young is frustrated and under pressure to get the class working effectively. Will and Kayla haven't brought their text to class, Jake, Syd and Josh are playing games on their ipads and Miss Young is busy getting Rob, Dean and Jack working on a modified Algebra program. While she is busy with them, the rest of the class becomes noisy with many students not working and amusing themselves by talking about off topic subjects like, who said what to whom on Facebook and who is going to be missing from the football side next Saturday.

Miss Young notices Beth using her mobile phone and retrieves it from her and puts it in the phone basket. Beth is clearly not amused so when Miss Young decides to lecture Beth about the new school policy for mobile phones, tears flow and Beth complains bitterly how she needs her phone and how unfair Miss Young is.

Tom is out of his seat and seems particularly boisterous today bouncing around the room chatting with his mates and distracting Julia from her work by drawing on her calculator.

There is a general restlessness in the classroom and the kids who are attempting to work, like Alli, Tran and Julia, are being distracted, and the kids who aren't working are happy just 'chillin'. "Miss, when are we ever going to use this?" Abe shouts over the top of all the noise and there is a general murmur of agreement from across the room. Miss Young responds with a burst about the noise level and then sarcastically comments to Abe that, "You're probably right for what you're going to end up doing."

Danni is noticeably quiet today but Miss Young doesn't get time to have a chat to her because she is constantly darting from one disengaged student to another in an attempt to keep them on task. Although determined to get the group working productively, Miss Young is fighting a losing battle. As soon as she gets one student working and moves to the next, the last student she helped becomes distracted and is off task again. As the period wears on, Miss Young feels like she is on a merry-go-round as she hurries from student to student valiantly trying to keep them working. She threatens the class with more homework and a lunch detention.

Finally, the bell rings and there is a stampede of tangled arms, legs, bodies and books as the class bolts for the door and on to their lockers before heading for home.

Teaching in the 21st century is not an easy job despite what the general the public might perceive about a job that comes with 10 weeks holiday and generous pay. Teachers today are under more pressure and more stress than ever before. Granted, my year nine example seems to be one of the most difficult cohorts of students to teach, but a discussion with any teacher at any level of education would reveal they have experienced a good range of the student issues that Miss Young faced in her Year 9 class.

"I have been teaching for over 25 years and I have faced a lot of challenges in my career and seen a lot of change. As a secondary teacher I find getting to know all your students well and being able to cater for their different needs is very challenging. We can have as many as 100-150 students in our classes in a year, so being able to know them all and differentiate so that their learning is meaningful to them is really challenging. Demands on teachers time has increased. There is more accountability, more targets, more paperwork, more PD, more meetings, more committees, more school events, more contact with parents, more excursions, more subjects, more technology, more pressure.

Without a doubt I think that managing time, stress and the demands of the job is the most challenging aspect of being a teacher." (Deb Derrick 2014 ASG National Excellence in Teaching Awards National Award Recipient)

What we have just witnessed is a normal everyday lesson for Miss Young's class and as a result she has worked herself into a lather of self doubt about the problems she faces in teaching. She complains bitterly to anyone who will listen about her problems:

- "Tom just gets to me. He wanders around, distracts other kids and is openly defiant." Despite her best efforts to control Tom, Miss Young knows that Tom is winding her up and she openly admits defeat and argues that if Tom doesn't want to learn in her classroom, "then this school is not the place for him." It has come to a point where Miss Young allows Tom to put her into a negative state of mind as soon as he walks into the classroom.

- "Jack and Will are so lazy they won't even try." They spend their lesson destroying pages in their workbook to build paper hats or airplanes, sticky taping pencils together and pulling highlighters to bits.

- "I'm not trained to teach kids like Dean. I can't be expected to cater for his needs when I have 23 other students in the room to look after." Dean is diagnosed with Motor Dyspraxia and Non-Verbal Learning Disabilities. Dean works on an Individual Learning Plan with specific instructions as to how he learns best and how to overcome his weak areas. Miss Young provides a modified program for Dean but it is simply a booklet of worksheets. It is a visual presentation of Dean's work when Dean has a diagnosed weakness for visual spacial relationships. His student notes clearly show that Dean finds written language a real challenge and requires verbal instructions to help him understand his school work. Yet Dean's modified work is visually presented.

- "I am embarrassed that I can't help Danni. I feel really guilty because all my time is taken up trying to manage Tom and get some work out of the likes of Jack and Meg and there are so many others." Danni is a quiet girl who tries hard but has several learning disabilities and finds maths a real challenge.

- "I'm sick of Will never bringing his text or work book to class. How can I teach a kid who can't even bring his books to class?"

- "Ben hasn't even completed 3.1 yet. He is never here so what hope have I got with a kid who only turns up every second lesson."

- "This class has missed three periods of maths in the last fortnight. First there was ANZAC Day, then parent - teacher interviews and this week the athletic sports. They have Year 9 camp in a fortnight and it just goes on. There is so much to do and I am continually robbed of our time."

- "I'm sick and tired of our technology not working. Either the internet is down, the projector won't work or the kids can't access the apps we need."

Throw in pressures from outside the classroom like:

- staff meetings, morning briefings, house meetings, faculty meetings, professional learning meetings

- training upgrades for First Aid, Mandatory Reporting, EpiPen, Emergency Evacuation procedures, lockdown procedures

- meeting and communicating with parents

- making the next student reporting deadline

- teacher performance review sessions

- camps and excursions and sporting activities

- complying with professional learning requirements

… and you will get some idea of what teachers like Miss Young are dealing with today.

Cassie Young feels like she is under siege from all directions. She blames the kids and the system, makes excuses for herself and denies that she can be part of the solution. There is a very high chance she will join the exodus of young teachers from their chosen profession. "Close to 50% of Australians who graduate as teachers leave the profession within the first five years." (Rebecca Vukovic Australian Teacher Magazine September 2015) That seems like a terrible waste of resources to me.

English research recently reported that 38% of teachers surveyed had seen a rise in mental health issues among colleagues in the past two years and 55% said their job had a negative impact on their own mental health. So Miss Young is not on her own because teachers all across Australia, and even overseas, are feeling the pressure and when that happens the kids' education suffers.

Just in case you don't believe me, let's take a look at these leading educational indicators:

- The Australian Bureau of Statistics estimates that 7.3 million Australians, or almost half the adult population, **do not have the functional literacy skills** to function effectively in modern society. These people often struggle to hold down jobs, balance their household budget and understand the mountains of paperwork we are all faced with. If Australian Education was doing its job, we would never achieve a statistic like this.

- PISA rankings for Australian students have slipped consistently over the past 20 years. "**AUSTRALIAN teenagers' reading and maths skills have fallen so far in a decade that nearly half lack basic**

maths skills and a third are practically illiterate. The dumbing down of a generation of Australian teenagers is exposed in the latest global report card on 15-year-olds' academic performance. Migrant children trumped Australian-born kids while girls dragged down the national performance in maths," the 2012 Programme for International Student Assessment (PISA) report, reveals. "Australia's maths performance dropped the equivalent of half a year of schooling between 2003 and 2012. And rowdy classrooms and bullying are more common in Australia than overseas," the report says.

- "Around 75,000 students in Years 3, 5, 7 and 9 who sat the NAPLAN tests last year **were not meeting national minimum standards.**" (Neil Garrett former Minister for Education)

- NAPLAN results indicate **consistently dropping achievement levels** in Reading, Writing and Maths. Federal Education Minister Christopher Pyne said, "Australia's results had declined despite a 44% increase in education spending over the past decade."

- The outlook is even worse for our disadvantaged kids from lower-income families who can be **up to three years behind their peers** by the time they enter Year 9.

- Our **indigenous students are on average two to three years behind** their classmates in reading by Year 9.

We shouldn't be proud of these statistics and as a country, we certainly shouldn't ignore them.

But what can those of us at the bottom of the education tree do? Our politicians have us heading in entirely the wrong direction and there seems to be little we can do.

The whole grass roots education school system is being overwhelmed by 'top down' pressure from the administration and our politicians. Education

has become a popular hot issue at election time and, because it is funded by Federal and State money, and because pretty much all voters have a vested interest in education, our politicians seem to think they should use education as a political vote catching issue to help get themselves re elected. Each new government tries to put their new stamp on education and they promise all manner of reforms designed to attract votes.

Election after election comes along bringing a whole new round of vote catching policy. Over the years they have come up with cycle after cycle after cycle of reforms and restructures: Schools of the Future, No Child Left Behind, An Even Start, BER (Building the Education Revolution), every child has a laptop and more recently the Higher Education Reform Bill, are all top down initiatives driven by politics. And while all this overbearing reform and restructure has been taking place, the educational outcomes for students and the working environment for teachers has deteriorated.

I wonder if our politicians have ever stopped to talk to the kids about how they feel about their education? If they did they would hear comments like these:

- "School is just plain boring. We don't learn any stuff that interests me." (Year 9 boy)

- "I hate all the homework and no one ever looks at it so I don't know why I bother with it." (Year 11 girl)

- "Why can't we learn practical stuff we are going to need to know like how to get a loan?" (Year 12 girl)

- "School sucks and the school doesn't care." (Year 9 boy)

Over the years our politicians have manacled those who work in education with a political correctness that has stifled a lot of the creativity we need in our classrooms. A good example is how Big Brother decrees that primary schools must spend the first two hours of every day on Literacy and the next hour and a half on Numeracy. But we saw LOTE (Languages Other Than English) become compulsory even though many schools couldn't source the staff to effectively deliver the subject, The Even Start remedial tutoring program came out with instructions that tutors should have no physical contact with students (not even shaking hands) and a gender neutral approach to teaching became the expected even though just about everyone agrees that boys and girls are different.

Teachers, and even our principals, are discouraged to speak out about the issues they have to contend with. Our politicians just don't seem to understand how debilitating this top down policy becomes to those at the heart of education. They ignore the fact that the very essence of education is the three way relationship between the parent, the student and the teacher and focus authoritarian means of improving PISA rankings, NAPLAN results and truancy rates. They are taking education down the wrong track completely and our kids are the ones that are suffering.

Yet, despite all this political interference and 'we know best' attitude, day after day, week after week, year after year, our teachers front up to work and do their best to meet the mounting challenges in our classrooms. Despite the fact that they feel they are under siege from all directions, they soldier on. But as Deb Derrick said, they are feeling tired and frustrated and battle weary and when that happens, the natural human reaction is to go into survival mode and just start going through the motions.

Some teachers do not survive, especially the young ones. Other teachers cling to their jobs because, like everyone else, they need the money and they don't know what else they would do. Some get to a point like Cassie Young in her Year 9 maths class where, despite her best efforts, very little student learning happens. Unfortunately, it is rare to find students excited about being at school these days, especially in our secondary schools. Thousands of students drop out of school every year and even more unhappy and disengaged students remain at school and don't achieve anywhere near their potential. Our student performance standards are dropping, student mental health is deteriorating, student engagement is at an all time low and all this despite the very best efforts from our teachers.

So what can we do?

Making excuses, denying there is a problem and blaming others is not going to help.

I believe we can and should reshape education from the ground up. I believe our teachers are in the best position to improve the educational outcomes for our kids. I believe it is the responsibility of school leaders, education leaders and political leaders to create a climate in education where our teachers have the best chance to improve the educational outcomes for our kids. And that now includes my grandkids.

A wonderful thing happened in my life on the 13th September 2013. I'm not sure if there is any significance in the symmetry of the numbers, 13 - 9 - 13, but it was a day my life changed.

That was the day my first grandson was born to my eldest son and his wife. Within five months my second grandson was born, a precious first child for my daughter and her husband and another precious grandchild for me.

For someone who has worked in and around education for most of my working life, the births of my two grandsons stirred a worrying thought inside me. At first I couldn't put my finger on what it was, but finally it hit me like a bucket of ice-cold water. Here were two helpless little human beings who would inevitably go off to school to be educated in a system that has at best struggled along since I first got involved as a four year old 57 years ago. But since the turn of the century the system has become less and less relevant to our students as they struggle to cope with a bewildering range of issues that I didn't have to contend with as a student.

Underpinning the life success and happiness of my grandkids will be the quality of their education. That success will largely come down to them being effectively educated by passionate and competent teachers; teachers who understand how to empower kids, how to sustain the flame of learning in them, and how to develop successful personal habits which support their physical, emotional, psychological and academic development for their future.

I am not interested in a school system which measures its success on NAPLAN results, ATAR scores and PISA rankings. I don't give two hoots if my grandkids can compete academically with other kids in England, New York or Tokyo. What I care about is how well equipped my grandkids will be to thrive throughout the 21st century. As I write this, two more grandkids are preparing for their entry into this world. There is no doubt that academic skills and abilities will be part of their building blocks for success. It will be handy if they learn to read effectively, write in a coherent manner and compute competently with numbers.

But much more important will be:

- how well they understand themselves and their purpose in this world

- how well they understand others, especially the opposite sex

- how well they can communicate, with themselves, with others and with their ever changing world

- how well they can think creatively, logically, structurally and flexibly

- how well they can look after themselves physically, mentally, socially and emotionally and keep their lives in balance

- how motivated they are to succeed and continue learning.

Cloe Madannes from the Madannes Institute in the US says, *"You don't need a PhD to change a life. You only need the right strategies."*

I don't have a PhD, a Masters or a career in educational research. What I have is a tattered, out of date, 1974 model, Diploma of Primary Teaching. My expertise, my tools, my strategies come from working with kids at the coalface of education. This includes kids from Prep to Year 12, white kids, black kids, Asian kids, disabled kids, smart kids, strugglers, special needs kids, kids off farms and town kids have all been part of my life over the last 40 odd years.

They don't care what piece of paper (qualification) we can wave at them from the front of the classroom. What they care about is how well we connect with them, how skilled we are at managing their classes, how well we challenge and ignite their learning, how gentle and supportive we are with their dreams, how passionate we are about their welfare and how adept we are at meeting their individual needs to find their place in the world.

There is some wonderful work being done in education and some of it is being done by those with a PhD. But, *"Passion doesn't always come with a PhD."* (Debra Woods, Life Fulfillment Coaching) and it is passion for the task that we really need.

I want my grandkids passionate and excited about their school and I want them taught by passionate and inspiring teachers. I want them to sing, to laugh, to play and to learn deeply some life lessons which will help them thrive to the end of this century. I want their teachers to build character in them, to challenge them and to acknowledge what they can do, not what they can't do.

This book aims at giving hope and purpose back to classroom teachers. If I tread on a few toes along the way, I'm sorry. Teachers are the ones at the coalface of education who can best reshape education for our kids and it's about time we got in and helped them instead of wrapping them up in bureaucratic red tape and political correctness. They've got a tough job to do but it is not impossible especially if Miss Young's journey of self discovery throughout this book gives them the odd tool or strategy to help them make a difference.

Chapter One

Mindmatters For Teachers

> "Attitude is a little thing that makes a big difference."
>
> (Winston Churchill)

Chapter One

Mindmatters For Teachers

When Cassie's Year 9 maths class is over, she heads back to her office feeling totally drained. She knows the class has not gone well, that student behaviour had been out of control and that her group is falling further and further behind the other Year 9 maths groups. She knows that some students were not happy with all the noise and distractions and she is resigned to more complaints from parents. Cassie is beside herself with worry and is her own harshest critic. She berates herself with statements like, "My classes are always noisy and behind while Pete's class is always so well behaved," and she second-guesses herself with questions like, "What am I doing wrong?" and "Why don't I teach like I used to?"

In desperation Cassie seeks out her mentor Todd and asks can she have a chat.

Todd can see from Cassie's body language that she is tense, agitated and in a very negative state of mind so he suggests they go for a walk.

Todd knows that Cassie cannot be counselled effectively while she is in such a pessimistic mental state. From her flushed face, nervous, darting eye movement and self-critical dialogue, Todd knows that Cassie's brain has gone into a 'flight or fight' response where the brain secretes a cocktail of hormones that will take 15-20 minutes to dissipate. This is a normal physical reaction to mental stress so light physical exercise such as walking is the first strategy Todd uses to help Cassie retreat from her flight or fight state of mind. Only then can he help her to see her situation in a more considered way and then to look for some solutions.

As they commence their walk, Todd opens the conversation by asking Cassie how her netball team is performing at the moment. This is the last question she expects but Todd knows that Cassie loves coaching the local Under 15 netball team so he is using this question to get Cassie's mind away from school and

into a more positive frame of mind. He listens intently as Cassie talks about her team's last match which ended in a narrow loss to the top team.

Todd then asks if there was anything funny that happened during that match. Spontaneously, Cassie starts laughing as she relates how an eighteen month old toddler had interrupted the match by wandering onto the court expecting to play netball with her big sister. (Todd knows that laughter is one of the quickest ways to change state in our bodies so he has found a way to make Cassie laugh).

As they continue their walk, Todd can start to see the physical changes in Cassie's body. Her face has relaxed and lost its flushed colour, she is smiling and relaxed and she is happily chatting away about kids and netball. Todd offers to buy Cassie a hot drink so they can sit quietly together to discuss why Cassie's maths class is causing her so much grief. With a coffee in hand they find a quiet table to examine what is happening in class.

Todd commences the conversation by using an open question such as, "You mentioned you are having some problems with your Year 9 maths class. Can you describe what is happening?"

He then listens keenly as Cassie starts to explain the key problems that she is experiencing:

- "My class is always noisy compared to Pete's class."

- "Tom is making me so mad. How can I teach well when he is wandering around annoying the other kids? If Tom doesn't want to learn then this school isn't for him."

- "I'm always behind at getting through the topics. I was a fortnight late finishing the Measurement topic and now I'm three weeks late in Algebra. I've missed a heap of classes through holidays and camps and sports days and I just can't make up the time."

- "There are kids in this class who won't even try. They don't even attempt the topic tests and this reflects poorly on my teaching because these kids won't have a go."

- "I provide a modified program for Rob and Jack and Dean but they just don't get it. I'm not trained to teach kids with Autism and I can't ignore the rest of the class to give them any more of my time."

- "And then there's Danni who tries so hard but needs constant help. I feel guilty because I haven't got the time to help her."

- "Will and Kayla never bring their books to class so how am I supposed to teach them?"

- "Felicity has missed so much school she hasn't even finished 3.1. She's got a lot of potential but she just keeps missing school."

- "What am I going to do?"

When Cassie has talked herself out, Todd paraphrases the problems she has outlined with, "So what I'm hearing is that you are feeling badly because your class is noisy and behind schedule due to things like missed lessons and kids missing school. You also sound concerned that you have kids in your class that you cannot help with their learning and in general the class is not learning the way you would like them to. Does that sound right?"

Cassie: "Yes that pretty much sums it up but what can I do?"

Todd: "We'll get to that but first, are there any other problems you can think of?"

Cassie: "Look I'm just sick of all the meetings and all the pressure. I hate myself and my job at the moment and I'm just so tired I'm over it."

Todd: "So apart from the problems you're experiencing in class, there are other pressures that have you feeling tired and hating yourself. Is that correct?"

Cassie sobbing: "I just don't know what to do."

Todd: "Well, you have already taken the first step by asking for help. Now that you have acknowledged you have a problem and asked for some help, it sounds like you are ready to take responsibility for where you are at and where you want to be."

Cassie: "What do you mean?"

Todd: "You may not have noticed this but you have been operating at what I call 'below the magic line'. It sounds to me that you are now ready to attempt to get yourself above the magic line. You have heard about the magic line haven't you?"

Cassie: "No!"

Todd: "Then let me explain on here."

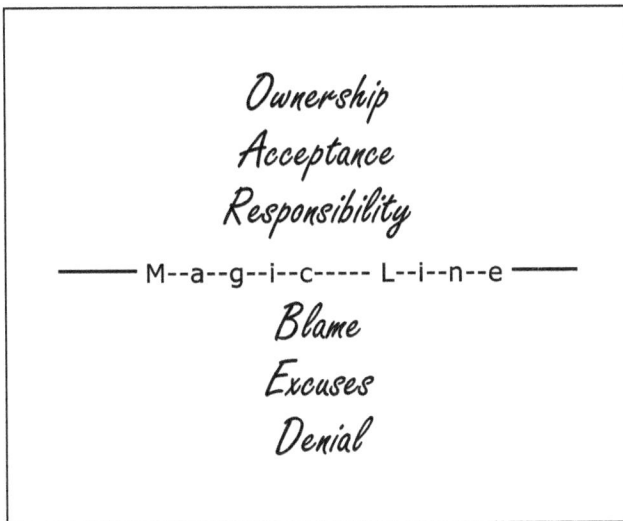

Ownership

Acceptance

Responsibility

——— M--a--g--i--c----- L--i--n--e ———

Blame

Excuses

Denial

Todd: "Up until now, and even at times tonight, where do you think you have been operating, above or below the magic line?"

Cassie: "Would it be mostly below the magic line?"

Todd: "I tend to think it is. From what I've heard you say, you have been blaming the kids and their parents, making excuses for yourself, and denying that you are part of the problem. The problem isn't your lack of skills or training and you are one of the most passionate, hard working and caring teachers I know. The problem is you have allowed yourself to choose to operate below the magic line. But tonight, it sounds to me like you have decided to take more ownership of the problem, to accept it and to take more responsibility for improving it. Tonight, you have decided you have had enough of being a victim and have taken the first step towards becoming a victor."

Cassie: "Wow, I never realised that I had become so negative. Was it really that bad?"

Todd: "Well what do you think?"

Cassie: "Yes, you are right, I have been whinging to everybody and I haven't wanted to admit I was part of the problem."

Todd: "That's right, and we all do that at times and so do the kids. If you can learn how to operate above the magic line, you can help your students to work there as well. Then magic things start to happen. So, are you ready for the next step?"

Cassie: "Absolutely, where do we start?"

Todd: "We start by looking at what has worked well for you in the past. But first, you have outlined a number of problems here. I want you to have a go at ranking them from least important to most important."

1	Noisy class
2	Tom
4	Behind the other Year 9s
1	Kids won't try
3	Not trained for special needs kids
6	No time for Danni
5	Kids won't bring text books
7	Kids missing school

Todd: "Okay, you have identified disinterested and noisy kids as the most important problems and they are closely related. How would you feel if we worked on that problem first?"

Cassie: "That would be great!"

Todd: "Okay, let's continue. What have you tried in the past that has worked well at engaging kids and when they were engaged, were they noisy and distracting?"

Cassie: "Well, when I was at my last school, I used to use a lot more practical, hands-on activities instead of relying on the text. It probably was noisy but the kids were busy and engaged in what they were doing and they were learning."

Todd: "Okay, would you say a more kinesthetic approach to teaching worked better for you and for the kids?"

Cassie: "Yes I would and now I think of it, I saw a teacher in my teaching rounds who was excellent at hands-on teaching of maths. I think I still have her phone number so I could give her a call."

Todd: "Fantastic, we already have two strategies you could use that you know have worked. What else?"

Cassie: "I'd like to learn more about applying maths to the real world. Maybe I could look for some PD that would help."

Todd: "Yeah, anything else?"

Cassie: "There are lots of maths programs and new apps out that might help."

Todd: "Absolutely, what else?"

Cassie: "I'm not sure, can you think of anything?"

Todd: "It's important that you come up with your own solutions but I wonder if it would be worth you talking to the maths faculty?"

Cassie: "That's a good idea, there is a lot of experience there."

Todd: "Okay so we have some tried and true hands-on teaching activities, a former colleague who is skilled at teaching maths kinesthetically, some targeted maths PD, utilising technology and chatting to the maths faculty. Which of those solutions do you feel will best give you the results you are looking for?"

Cassie: "Definitely using some of my old hands-on teaching activities but I also like the idea of doing some PD on the latest technology available for teaching maths."

Todd: "Okay, let's write a goal around those two solutions. We start by writing a goal that you have already achieved in the future. When would you like to have achieved this goal?"

Cassie: "By the end on this month."

Todd: "Okay, write the goal as though it is now the end of the month and you have just achieved your goal."

Friday 13th February

It is now three thirty on Friday the Twenty Seventh of February 2015 and I have just packed up from running the most amazing lesson where the kids were totally engaged in learning Algebra and the strategies and tools I learnt at last week's PD worked beautifully. I feel so relieved and inspired and excited at what the kids are learning and I feel proud to be their teacher.

Steps I need to take to achieve my goal:

1. Research PDs available and choose one   by   Tuesday 17th February

2. Get approval from PD coordinator   by   Thursday 19th February

3. Book the PD   by   Friday 20th February

4. Attend the PD when it runs

5. Dig out my old lesson plans for Algebra   by   Sunday 22nd February

6. Choose three hands on activities to try with the kids

7. Get any aids and resources I need   by   Tuesday 24th February

8. Implement the activities and PD learning   by   Friday 27th February

Obstacles

- Can't find the aids I need
- No suitable PDs

Back up plan

Ask Maths faculty to purchase

Search for YouTube tutorials

Who do I need to assist me?

1. Todd to keep me accountable for my goals

2. PD coordinator for PD approval

How strong is my intention to take the first step?   1 2 3 4 5 6 7 8 ⑨ 10

How strong is my enthusiasm to take the first step?   1 2 3 4 5 6 7 8 9 ⑩

How strong is my commitment to take the first step?   1 2 3 4 5 6 7 8 ⑨ 10

Todd: "Fantastic, you are on your way to becoming a victor."

"A teacher's mindset is their greatest asset or their greatest liability. There is no right or wrong way to teach. What works for some, doesn't work for others, but it is the teacher's mindset that makes the difference with the kids."

(Ian Davies)

Essential Teacher Mindset Tools

Mindset is the way we think about our world. It includes our thoughts, beliefs, ideas and attitudes that shape how we think about ourselves and the world we live in. Our mindset determines how we behave, how we approach life and how we operate in the classroom. We can all get stuck in our mindset at times but luckily, we can also easily shift our mindset if we choose to. That is what Cassie did when she decided to approach Todd for some help. She chose to shift her mindset from that of a victim with a fixed mindset stuck blaming, making excuses and in denial, to that of a victor with a proactive growth mindset operating above the magic line.

The development of a growth mindset can be best covered by dealing with these six essential areas:

1. Leading Yourself

Teachers are automatically put into a leadership role whether they like it or not. Students, parents and the community expect teachers to be leaders and role models for the kids they work with. The first step for anyone to become an effective leader is to learn to lead themselves and that applies to teachers as well. It's all about self development and the following points explore this.

A key self communication tool is learning to tame and control that little voice inside our head that keeps telling us what we can or cannot do. For many teachers our teaching dreams get lost in the frustrations and routines of

everyday school life and that little voice turns negative on us by telling us things like, "What am I doing wrong?" or "Why can't I teach as well as Pete?"

One of the simple ways to turn our negative thoughts into more positive thoughts is to ask ourselves **better quality questions**. Instead of Miss Young asking, "Why can't I control Tom's behaviour?" she could learn to ask more empowering questions such as, "Why can't I control Tom's behaviour **yet**?" or even, "How can I control Tom's behaviour and have fun with him at the same time?" These new questions suddenly become more empowering. There's hope there now and the mindset is automatically activated to look for ways to improve Tom's behaviour in the classroom.

As Eli Weisel puts it,

> "every question possesses the power that is lost in the answer. The real answers you will find only within yourself."

Another way to reframe negative thoughts is to simply think positive and reinforce those thoughts with simple messages such as:

- Every day in every way my teaching is getting better and better
- Every day in every way I wake up a better teacher than yesterday
- Every day in every way I am learning more and more about kids

As Walter Whittle puts it in his poem, **If You Think:**

If you think you are beaten, you are

If you think you dare, you don't!

If you want to win, but think you can't, you won't

If you think you'll lose, you're lost;

For out in the world

We find Success begins with a fellow's will;

It's all in the state of mind.

Life's battles don't always go

To the stronger and faster man

But sooner or later the man who wins

Is the man who thinks he can

The second key to self communication is to understand **choice**. We all have the power to choose how we react to any situation and the meaning we give to it. Miss Cassie Young chose to be a victim to all the issues her students were bringing to her classroom and to operate below the Magic Line. It was only when she changed her choice to that of a victor above the magic line that she started to turn her teaching around.

The third key to self communication is to be **grateful**. Being grateful is all about acknowledging yourself and those around you when good things happen to you. Simple affirmation statements starting with, "I am grateful for …." enrich your life and help you communicate with yourself in a positive and supporting way.

My preference is to finish the, "I am grateful for…" sentence at least 10 times each morning while I go for my morning walk. But there are many other ways to achieve the same thing. Some write it in their journal, others sing it, others write a list. It is your choice how you do it but it is essential you acknowledge with yourself how grateful you are to be making a difference in kids' lives.

2. Understanding Your Strengths and Weaknesses

The second step to leading yourself is to learn and understand that we all have strengths and weaknesses, abilities and disabilities. It helps if we are aware of our strengths and weaknesses because then we are in a position to make some decisions about them. For example, do I work on improving a strength or do I work on compensating for a weakness? This is a good question for us all to ponder on. One of my strengths is my ability to connect with kids. One of my disabilities is I struggle with face recognition. I can walk past my own wife if she is mixed up in a crowd of people.

Write down three of your strengths here:

- _____

- _____

- _____

And now, write down three of your weaknesses here:

*   _____

*   _____

*   _____

Now that you have your strengths and weaknesses down on paper, what's one thing you could do to improve yourself as a leader of children?

I could write a goal to _____

and that would mean _____

Now all you have to do is go to the www.DynamicTeachingTools.com website to download a free Goal Setting template and you can have your goal underway today.

And when will you have that done by? I will have that done by: _____/_____/_____

See how self awareness of our strengths and weaknesses makes it easier to change them.

It can be that easy for your students as well.

3. Selecting Your Team

Your team is the people you surround yourself with who can challenge you, support you and inspire you. Choose carefully who you put in your team. Your family, your friends, your peer group, even your fellow teachers can be a huge barrier for you if, for whatever reason, they are disempowering you or leading you into trouble.

We can't choose our family; we just have to love them for who they are. But we do have the choice as to which members of our family we pick for our team.

Look for family members who will help to challenge you and help you grow and contribute.

The same applies to your peer group and friends. Choosing the peer group you identify with is a critical key to your success. The same applies with your friends. True friends will support you to follow your dreams but there is a trap with many friendships. If you have friends in your team that don't support you in the direction you want to go, they will subconsciously (or maybe even consciously) find ways to undermine your dreams and goals. The reason for this is because we all have a basic need to feel significant, and if you start to shine, your family and friends might feel you are leaving them behind and that makes them feel insignificant because they will compare themself to you. So they'll make disempowering comments and subconsciously do things to try and hold you at their level.

Write down 6 people you feel will be good for your team:

1. _____ because _____

2. _____ because _____

3. _____ because _____

4. _____ because _____

5. _____ because _____

6. _____ because _____

As the leader of your team, try to find ways to support the people that are supporting you. Think for a moment how you can show your support for your team and show your gratitude to them. Then write down what you are going to do to look after the members of your team.

I am going to _____

and _____

Apart from the team you have consciously selected, you also have a subconscious team working for you 24 hours a day. This team keeps the basics going like keeping your heart ticking and you breathing. But there is more to our subconscious than that. It also is responsible for many of our habits both good and bad and many of the scripts we run in our head. Our subconscious team can be trained up and redirected like our conscious mind. In fact if our conscious thoughts are in conflict with our sub conscious thoughts we will find it impossible to operate effectively. Aligning our conscious and subconscious thoughts is crucial to effective self management.

Here's a strategy to help you achieve this. It is a bit spooky but I recommend you give it a try and experience the joy of bringing positive change to your life.

Find a spot where you are really comfortable and yet private. Take a seat and close your eyes.

As you breathe in, imagine a rush of beautiful fresh air entering your body through the soles of your feet. Practise breathing in deeply so that you can feel the wonderful fresh air rising up through your body and right to the top of your head.

Hold your breath briefly and then breathe out through the soles of your feet. But now you are not breathing out fresh air, now image you are breathing out all the tension, worries, negativity and stale air in your body. Completely empty your body of air.

Repeat breathing in fresh air and breathing out the stale air through the soles of your feet until you feel totally relaxed and re energised.

Now I want you to image that you are sitting at your classroom desk and I want you to invite into your imaginary classroom all the people who represent you and your subconscious mind. Invite in your heart expert, your breathing master, your sex guru, your motivation trainer, your self defence expert and so on until you have everyone at your kitchen table. I like to give all my subconscious team a name so that I can go around my team, one by one, to thank them for coming in and for all the work they do to keep me safe and alive and functioning. Do that now with each member of your team.

Next I would like you to explain to your team that you regret not having connected with them regularly in the past to acknowledge all their great work and that from now on you are going to change that and acknowledge and support them every day. Also explain your vision for the future, how you wish to make changes in your life. Explain how getting everyone working together with clear direction and support will mean many of the old problems like procrastination and self doubt will disappear and a new, focused you will emerge.

Share with your team what you really want to happen in your life and go around the team one by one explaining what you need them to do. Ask them to give you a sign that you have their commitment and support. If any of your team seem reluctant, explain to them how important it is that they all work together and negotiate with them until you have their support for the new future that you wish to create. Ask your team to give you a conscious sign every morning as you prepare for another school day that they are happy and focused on working together with you and the rest of the team to achieve your goals.

Repeat this exercise each day and celebrate your changes, successes and achievements with your team.

4. Be Coached

Being coached by a proficient coach is a vital tool for teachers and especially beginner teachers. To be coached or mentored by someone who you can confide in and who can give you support when you feel you need it can be the difference between success and failure. Being coached helps give you an operating manual, not only for your teaching, but your life in general.

Most of the really successful people in the world are coached or mentored. This includes business coaching, sports coaching, corporate coaching, wellbeing coaching and teacher coaching. If you want to improve your tennis, you get coached and practice applying what they teach you.

It's the same with teaching. Find yourself a coach and practice what you learn and you will have to improve.

There are lots of ways for teachers to be coached these days:

- Personal coaching by a Life Coach who understands teaching
- Working with a mentor from within your school
- Online coaching
- Coaching DVDs
- Self help books for teachers

5. Self Defense For Teachers

As we have already seen, teachers in the 21st century face many forms of disruptive behaviour from some of today's students who, most would agree, are becoming progressively more difficult to manage. Complaints of rude, disrespectful, lazy, disengaged and problem students rebound around the walls of staffrooms all across the country. Even the wider community has noticed some kids becoming more of a handful and treating adults with less respect than they expect.

Teachers like Miss Young can easily fall into the trap of seeing the student as the only problem. This approach ultimately leaves teachers with two unsatisfactory options:

1. Carry on regardless and ignore the problems because I'm not trained, I haven't the time or any one of a number of other excuses. Under this laissez faire approach students learn they have all the power and when that happens, the learning environment is sure to be less than optimal.

2. Implement the school's Discipline Policy which may well go something like this:

- first offense gets a warning
- second offense gets lunch time detention
- third offense means call in a House Leader, Wellbeing Coordinator or member from Leadership (Vice Principal or Principal), a call home and punitive action.

When teachers go down this authoritarian track, and that is what schools usually expect them to do, they end up like Miss Young back in her Year 9 maths class with a constant stream of self assured teenagers pushing the limits and becoming less and less tolerant of her authority.

But Miss Young, with Todd's help, is showing that there is another way to approach student learning and behaviour and we continue this theme of self help right throughout this book as we follow what she learns.

In her book, 'Coat Of Many Colours', Jenny Mackay tells a story from a teacher she came across that seemed to always have her class under control and working effectively. Jenny asked her what her secret was and this was her reply:

"I'll share it with you but you may only pass it on to someone who knows how to value such a thing. It's my invisible coat. I put it on every morning as I enter the school grounds. I walk around with it all day. I appreciate its calming effect. It keeps me sane and my stress levels down, it supports me and is reassuring, particularly when my students are giving me hassles and in the very rare times when I really need it, it keeps me safe. For this coat has a multitude of pockets and in every pocket there is a skill, a technique, a strategy. When I face a recalcitrant student, an annoying, irritating, challenging or rude student, I unzip a pocket and take out a skill.

I spend time adding pockets to this coat. When things have gone wrong in the day, or the lesson has not gone as it should have because of what students said or did, I ask myself, 'What was the possible reason for that and how will I manage a similar situation next time?' And in finding a solution, I add another pocket to my coat."

This is an alternative way of approaching student learning and classroom management. It is an 'above the magic line' approach and it helps protect a teacher's wellbeing.

A similar tool to the 'Coat of Many Colours' is called the Energy Shield. Every day and with every class teachers receive energy from the kids. Sometimes it is positive energy such as when we see students learning, when we receive great feedback, when kids get excited about learning or when parents acknowledge us for helping their kids.

Sometimes we receive negative energy from the class in the form of disruptive behaviour, rudeness, disrespect, anger and work refusal.

The Energy Shield gives teachers a choice for how they deal with the inevitable energy flowing into their persona from their class members. Miss Young has been choosing to take on board all the negative energy she feels from her Year 9 maths class and she has been using that energy to fuel her below the magic line mindset and behaviour.

On the other hand Miss Young has been overlooking any small amounts of positive energy the class has been offering her because all her mindset focuses on is bringing in the negative energy.

But what if she flipped her choice? What if she decided to deflect all the negative energy with her imaginary shield and accept every bit of positive energy she was offered, to give herself a pat on the back when things worked well and to fuel her motivation and self esteem with positive energy?

6. Keeping Your Life Balance Wheel Rolling

Teachers are no different to anyone else. They need to keep their life in balance. This is often difficult for teachers to achieve because they have such an emotional attachment to helping kids learn that they can sometimes spend too much time on school stuff and lose sight of their life balance.

It is crucial that teachers enter their classroom in good shape mentally, physically and socially. If they don't, their students will often suffer. The following life balance activity can help teachers like Miss Young to identify areas in her life balance that she might not be aware she is neglecting.

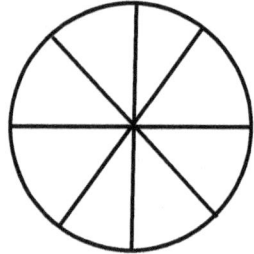

Let's describe to Miss Young how the Life Balance Wheel works:

Firstly, the wheel has 8 spokes representing each of the 8 areas of our life:

1. The Physical. How fit you are, how healthily you eat, how much you exercise
2. The Spiritual. How good you feel about yourself in the world, how connected you feel, how much you are growing as a person
3. The Career. How you feel about your job, your job prospects and your job security
4. The Finances. How financially secure you are, how content are you with your financial situation, how close to your financial goals you are
5. The Social. How you feel about your current social situation with friends and work mates, how much being socially accepted means to you
6. The Relationships. Your take on your current relationship status, how happy you are with your current partner, how close you are to your ideal partner

7. The Family. This can be tricky. Family is family whether you like them or not and we have to put up with them simply because they are family. But how do you see your family situation, are you happy with the time you spend with family and how many 'issues' do you have with them?
8. The Contribution. We all need to feel we are contributing to others. It is one of our basic human needs. So, how well are you meeting that need?

Each spoke is metered from 0 to 10 with 0 in the centre and 10 on the rim.

Your task is to rate where you fit on each spoke of the wheel from 0 to 10 where 0 is the lowest rating and 10 is the highest.

Once you have done that, join your ratings along the spokes to create a rim like this:

What sort of a ride do you think you would get if your Life Balance Wheel looked like this?

Life would be a pretty bumpy ride wouldn't it?

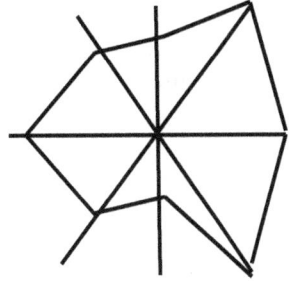

Completing the life balance activity helps us see where things are a bit flat in our lives. Once we understand this, then we can do something about it by setting some simple goals to inflate our low ratings, get our lives back in balance and have a much less bumpy ride.

Teaching is all about mindset. Once you understand how to bulletproof your mindset, there is no reason why you can't teach the same strategies to your students.

10 empowering assumptions about teaching:

1. Focusing on the positive facilitates change in the desired directions.
2. Exceptions help build solutions. Exceptions mean trying different ways of doing things.
3. Change is occurring all the time- nothing is always the same.
4. Small changes lead to larger changing.
5. When students show us how they think change occurs, cooperation is inevitable.
6. Students have all they need to solve their problems when they are resourceful. Our job as teachers is to generate understanding and encourage action and resourcefulness.
7. Meaning is created through our stories, interactions and experiences.
8. Learning is often circular.
9. The meaning of the message is the response you receive.
10. The student is the expert.

Chapter 1 Resources:

1. Go to the www.DynamicTeachingTools.com website to download a free Goal Setting template and you can have your goal underway today.

2. Aussie Kids Coach Leadership Workshop For Kids

3. Recommended Reading: 'Coat Of Many Colours', Jenny Mackay

Understanding Education For Kids

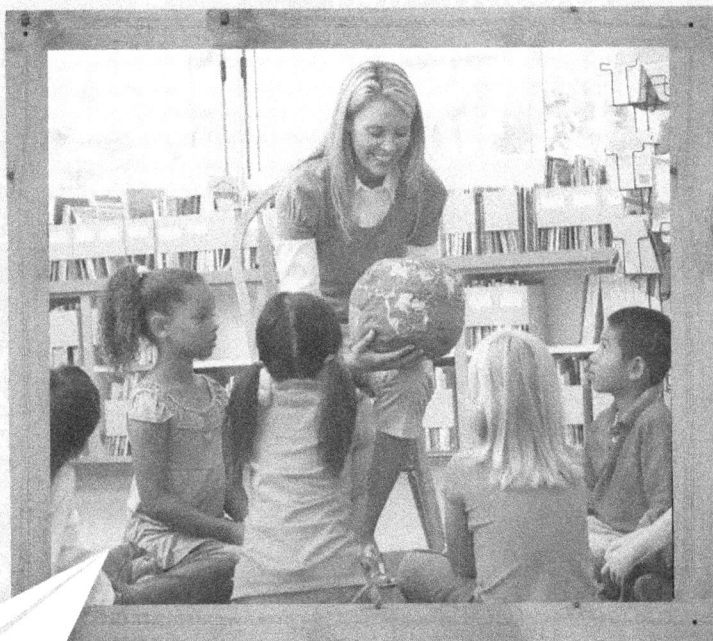

> "There is a genius inside every child and it is your job to help bring it out."
>
> **(Mary Egan, Ballarat Teacher's College)**

Chapter Two

Understanding Education For Kids

One of the first things that happened in my first year at Teacher's College was a program where all first year students were split up around the primary schools in Ballarat to run remedial reading classes with small groups of struggling readers. I ended up in the heart of the housing commission area at Wendouree West Primary School with a group of four grade three Koorie boys, who had as much interest in learning to read as I had in studying French at high school!

I wracked my brain to find a way to get these kids interested in reading and somehow I came up with an idea that worked. What these kids were interested in was Aussie Rules Football. They lived and breathed footy so I started creating reading activities using their interest in football as a basis. My activities were designed to teach these kids how the English language worked phonetically and it was pretty simple:

When we speak English we make sounds and there are 44 of them.
When we write English we write symbols for these sounds from our 26 letter alphabet and there are 73 of these symbols.
Learning to write means learning which letters to write for the sounds we speak.
Learning to read means learning which sounds to speak for the letters we see.
Sometimes we use one letter for a sound.
Sometimes we use two or more letters for a sound.

My remedial reading group learned how to sound out the names of their favourite players, even ones like D-e-s T-u-d-d-e-n-h-a-m. They learnt how to write simple sentences using words like tap and bump and kick and to spell words like ball, foot and hand.

The smile on those kids faces when they realised they were learning to read and write had a powerful impact on me. All of a sudden I knew I had discovered

one of the secrets to teaching: **kids learn well when they are interested in what they are learning.**

Forty odd years later I am still working at the grassroots level of education and I am still using this basic strategy to get disinterested, disengaged and frustrated kids to become interested in learning again.

The lessons I learnt with my remedial reading group were the most profound lessons in my teacher training. Admittedly, I learnt a bit about child development and Bloom's Taxonomy and I finally got excited about learning. I found I loved learning about psychology and so I majored in it and for the first time in my entire education, I excelled at a subject and achieved honors in my psychology major.

I also majored in mathematics and economics which were two obscure subjects for a primary school teacher, given that the maths course was basically a first year university maths course and economics was an extension of Form 6 Economics. I soon found out that they were not a great preparation for teaching children to read, how to compute with numbers and how to maintain a good learning environment in a classroom. To put it simply, my teacher training had been far short of ideal because I hadn't learnt why kids behave the way they do. I hadn't learnt that boys learn differently to girls. In fact I hadn't been taught much at all about how kids learn. It was mostly a blur of academic fluff that never did anything to prepare me for running a classroom, let alone running a school. Yes, that's right. Back in those days, many male graduates were sent into far flung and isolated rural areas as headmasters of the local rural school.

My first appointment was at Macorna Primary School where the academic progress of twenty three students across seven grades rested squarely on my novice shoulders. As well, I was responsible for all the departmental administrative work, the financial records, the phone calls, ordering supplies, the school committee, working with the mother's club, liaising with parents, the cleaning and whatever else came up.

My teacher training had not spent one minute preparing me for the administrative side of running a school so it is fair to say my first year out of Teacher's College was a huge learning curve.

However, two pearls of wisdom were left with me from Teachers College that did help me through that hectic first year. These thoughts were delivered by Mary Egan, a senior lecturer just before our third year group was to begin our final teaching rounds prior to graduation.

She sat down with us one day and told us two things:

"Despite our three years of training you in the modern ways of teaching, our research suggests that within three years you will teach the way you were taught."

Now as I have explained, I wasn't taught in ways that worked for me at my secondary school so this message hit home like a cartoon anvil and left me with a desire to make myself into a more effective teacher than the ones that had taught me. Do you know that after 40 years in education that thought is still a prime motivator for me?

The second thing Mary told us was:

**"There is a genius inside every child and it is your
job to help bring it out."**

Somehow this snapshot of a teacher's role also grew roots in me during that first year at Macorna. I had a great bunch of kids there but there were kids that struggled too. Dave was in grade one and hadn't yet grasped the relationship between the sounds we make and the letters we use to represent the sounds. Then there was Rommi, who was dyslexic in the same grade as Kylie who was 'flying', and a whole mix of kids from advanced grade six level down to preps. Mary's genius statement kept my expectations up for the struggling kids until I found a way of teaching them that worked for their learning styles and catered for their weaknesses and their strengths.

But I knew I had a lot to learn about kids; how they think, why they behave the way they do, and how they learn.

Miss Young was in the same boat with Tom the wanderer who is now in his tenth year of schooling and still struggles to read effectively. In maths class this means Tom can't read well enough to understand what the questions in his text book are asking him to do. So wandering the classroom had become a favourite and entrenched behaviour for Tom.

Miss Young can't understand why Tom behaves like this and has arrived at a stage where it is distracting her from her teaching. Tom meanwhile, knows exactly what he is doing. It is called attention seeking behaviour and Tom is a well practiced master at it. He knows it works beautifully on Miss Young. Every time he 'goes for a wander' Tom can see Miss Young's body language change; her face goes red, her hands and neck tense up and she starts to yell. Tom takes great power from being able to affect Miss Young like this. It makes him feel important and he is certain it will work. For a child like Tom who is getting no feeling of importance from his class work, winding up the teacher helps him satisfy his need for importance. It is a need we all share and it is a need we all satisfy in some way.

The Fundamentals Of Needs Based Psychology

This brings Miss Young to a lesson on needs based psychology. If we can help her understand what Tom is doing and why, we can help her help Tom to satisfy his need for significance in a more positive way.

Needs based psychology is founded on understanding why we humans behave the way we do. The thinking is that all of our behaviour is based on satisfying one or more of six basic needs that we all share.

I have these same six needs just the same as you and Tom and everyone else but we all satisfy them in ways that are unique to us. We need to understand that kids are like that too, from the well off child at Xavier College in Melbourne to the Koorie kid at Lajamanu in outback Australia. If Miss Young accepts and understands needs based psychology and applies it to her work with children, she can make an enormous difference in their lives.

Need 1. **The Need for Certainty**

Children need to feel safe, to avoid pain and to feel comfortable in the classroom. All children need to have some sense of certainty and security at school and some will find all sorts of weird vehicles to achieve their sense of security.

Some of the stranger vehicles for security I have seen are: must have a can of Coke in their lunchbox; must have their hair plaited exactly the same each day; must have their jade guitar pick in their wallet, but for most students a sense of security and certainty is achieved from:

- their friendship group
- where they sit in the classroom
- the rules that keep them safe and out of trouble as long as those rules are applied fairly and consistently
- seeing themselves learning successfully
- knowing they are respected and appreciated for their efforts
- receiving positive school reports.

Other students will satisfy their need for certainty in more negative ways, such as:

- telling themselves they are certain they are dumb and they are wasting their time even attempting their school work. The problem with these kids is, they aren't dumb; they just won't try hard enough to know how smart they are. They will never know how smart they are until they give their school work somewhere close to 100% effort but they get certainty and take comfort from identifying themselves as being dumb and by not having a go.

- being certain that they can push your buttons and disrupt the class and have some fun in the process. These are often the dare-devil kids who can't sit still and who love surprise, suspense and challenges. They are often quite creative in the way they can disrupt classroom proceedings and they get used to being in trouble. They will even take pride in their list of punishments they've received. Our friend Tom is a good example of students who achieve certainty like this.

- being certain they can get away with not working in class if they don't bring their text or work books. This is a common strategy for many students and they develop a long list of reasons as to why they can't seem to bring their books to class. Some of the more creative reasons I have heard are: Dad took it in the car when he went back to Warrnambool (blaming others); I didn't think we would need it today so I left it at home (denial); my boyfriend slept over last night (making excuses).

Teachers who understand this need can ensure it is provided for in their classrooms through:
- having a routine that students understand
- having a seating arrangement that provides the optimum support for the individual needs of the class members
- having two or three basic rules for behaviour management
- being firm, fair and consistent
- ensuring students can see they are learning
- ensuring all students actively participate during class.

Code words for certainty are: comfort, security, safety, stability, feeling grounded, predictability and protection.

Providing for certainty in the classroom is an important part of providing a workable learning environment. However, if students are too certain all the time, class life becomes dull and boring for students and teachers. Hence we come to the second basic need.

Need Two: **The Need for Uncertainty**

Some degree of certainty and routine in a classroom is essential but we get bored with too much certainty.

Consider this:

If the students in your class are certain they know exactly what is going to happen in class day after day after day, they will get bored. If the students in your class are asked to sit still and for hour after hour work on arithmetic, spelling or comprehension in their workbooks, don't be surprised if some of them start to fidget!

They are children, not adults. Some children do not have the attention span to sit passively at a desk for long periods of time doing the same thing.

So the second need teachers should provide for is uncertainty, in the form of:

- variety
- challenge
- suspense
- surprise
- fun
- excitement.

Incorporating uncertainty into lessons will stimulate the child's emotional, intellectual and physical wellbeing and will help prevent disruptive behaviour before it starts.

Uncertainty should become part of class routine because students caught in the same routine day after day will seek change and look for uncertainty, quite often at the expense of the teacher's classroom activities.

Students can instinctively achieve uncertainty in a positive way if a teacher encourages:

- new learning with a have-a-go attitude
- challenge and competition
- surprise and change
- the fun of learning new and interesting things in new and interesting ways
- suspense and intrigue.

Children need the excitement that comes from variety to feel alive and if teachers don't provide for it, students will, and most probably in the form of disruptive behavior, such as:

- playing games on their ipad/netbook
- distracting other students through talking, wandering, flicking wads of paper, etc
- entertaining themselves on their phone, doodling or any amount of other creative ways
- asking if they can go to the toilet/go for a drink/go to their locker for something they just realised they might need.

Code words for uncertainty/variety are: fear, instability, change, chaos, entertainment, suspense, exertion, surprise, conflict and crisis.

The need for uncertainty is a bit of a balancing act with the need for certainty because they are opposite fundamental needs. The next need is just as powerful.

Need Three: **The Need for Love and Connection**

Let me get this straight right from the start. While we all need love in our life, that does not mean teachers need to love their students. In fact, there will be some students they find very hard to even like. That is completely normal but that reality does not mean teachers can't provide for connection with every student. It really is very important for all children, especially for teenagers, to feel connected and even loners need to connect in some way with their peers and adults.

In its positive form, connection is achieved through:

- rapport developed by their teacher
- group activities, class discussions and working with a partner
- team activities and games
- friendships and friendship groups
- sport and interest groups
- boyfriends/girlfriends
- social media. Social media is very popular with kids of the 21st Century. It can be a distraction at times in the classroom but as we'll see in a later chapter, it can be a very powerful connection tool for teachers.

In its negative form, connection can be achieved through:

- bullying groups
- gangs
- gossip groups
- cyber bullying through social media.

Connection based activities are useful strategies for teachers to integrate into their lessons and thereby meet their students' need for connection in the classroom. The next need is the need to feel important.

Need Four: **The Need for Significance**

The need for significance is a fundamental personality need for all of us. Every person needs to feel important, needed, and wanted in some way. Provide for these three things in the classroom and Miss Young will go a long way towards improving student engagement and her classroom learning environment.

Teachers can use the need for significance to their advantage through helping students to achieve self importance in a whole range of positive ways, such as:

- doing neat work and being rewarded for it
- actively participating in class discussions and being acknowledged for it

- being responsible for something (for example, a monitor's job)
- building or creating something unique and presenting it to the class
- bringing something from home and being an expert on it to the class
- doing well on assessment tasks and thereby achieving a goal
- behaving in a respectful and responsible manner and being complimented for it.

However, if the need for significance is ignored in the classroom, students will find their own ways to meet this need through:

- being the class clown (which can be a positive if used in the right way) and disrupting classroom proceedings at the expense of other students and the teacher

- deliberately getting into trouble. You might be surprised know this actually empowers some children and it is easy for them to achieve in a 'command and control' style of classroom

- refusing to work. The passive resistor type student will feel important because they disempower the teacher's efforts to teach them and they know the teacher can do little about it

- bullying in all its forms empowers kids who make themselves feel important at the expense of other kids

- by tearing down something (vandalism) or someone (rumours, gossip, criticism).

Understanding how the need for significance affects kids in the classroom is a key learning for Miss Young and gives her the opportunity to assist her students to become self-motivated and equipped with the self-discipline and self-sufficiency tools to help them along the road to success.

Code words for significance are: pride, importance, standards, achievement, performance, perfection, evaluation, discipline, competition and rejection.

The above four needs are the needs of the personality. The following two needs are needs of the spirit and they also must be satisfied if kids are to remain spiritually happy and healthy.

Need Five: **The Need for Growth**

If human beings stop learning and growing as a person, they die in spirit and lose all purpose in life. The World Health Organisation (WHO) has predicted that by 2030, depression will account for the highest level of disability accorded any physical or mental disorder in the world (WHO, 2008).

Even in Australia today, "significant levels of depression affect approximately 20 per cent of adults either directly or indirectly during their lifetime, with almost twice as many women diagnosed with the disorder compared to men." (www.beyondblue.org.au) The cost to society is staggering. "Depression costs the Australian economy approximately $12.6 billion per year and accounts for up to six million working days of lost productivity, and there are significant personal and social costs to individuals and their families which are associated with depression." (www.beyondblue.org.au)

In his book, 'Man's Search For Meaning', Victor Frankl makes the observation that many of his psychology patients complain of "a feeling of the total and ultimate meaninglessness of their lives. They lack the awareness of a meaning worth living for. They are haunted by the experience of their inner emptiness."

This feeling of emptiness is prevalent in teenagers in our schools. They are at a stage in their lives where they challenge everything they are asked to do with questions and statements such as "When am I ever going to need this?", "What we learn is not important to me", and "I don't need to learn maths when I have a calculator."

Teachers can play a vital role of averting these dire predictions if they teach their students how to become self reliant at self growth.

How can they do that?

Basically it comes down to:

- helping to ignite the flame of learning in them through teaching to their interests
- taking time to explain how their learning applies to the real world
- using videos or guest speakers to help illustrate how their curriculum can help them prepare for adult life
- helping to 'bring out the genius' inside kids with a gentle word of encouragement or a delicate push towards their passion
- helping kids to understand themselves and their situation in life. They can understand if we explain to them that their brains are undergoing a major reconstruction that will not be complete until they are in their early to mid 20's.
- when they stress about subject selections we can encourage them to follow their passions and interests instead of sticking with their friends
- helping students to take ownership of their learning through giving them choice and a say in their assessment expectations.

Code words for growth are: developing, learning, self-improvement, studying, and understanding.

We now come to the final need.

Need Six: **The Need for Contribution**

A life is incomplete without the sense that one is making a contribution to others or to a cause. It is human nature to want to give back and to leave a mark on the world. In the adult world giving to others may take a multitude of forms and directions, such as giving time to community service, making a charitable donation, planting trees, writing a book or giving to one's children to name, just a few.

For school kids, the need for contribution may seem a little less important than the other five needs we have discussed. However, this need is a powerful ally for teachers to utilize in the classroom.

Many primary schools use a buddy system to help new students to settle into school. I found pairing senior students with junior students was a highly successful strategy when I worked in one-teacher rural schools. The senior students would read to their partner, listen to them read, play maths based games with them and buddy with them on excursions and sports days. It is difficult to measure the sense of contribution a student gains from mentoring another student but the feedback I got from them is that it was a very rewarding experience for them.

The buddy system used extensively in many primary schools doesn't seem to be utilised anywhere near as much in secondary school or at tertiary level. Other buddy tool applications include:

- Leadership Buddies where a senior leader mentors a more junior leader

- Teacher-Pupil Buddies where each student has a teacher buddy whom they see on a regular basis for help with any school issues

- New Chum Buddies where each new student at a school has an experienced buddy as a go-to person

- Teacher-Teacher Buddies where teachers are mentored by other teachers

- Sport Buddies who exercise and train together.

Helping students work for a cause outside the school is also a valuable vehicle to satisfy their juvenile need for contribution, for example, raising money for sick kids or less fortunate kids overseas can be supported by developing pen pals between kids who have never met each other. Projects like this give real world benefit to those less fortunate and real world sense of contribution to our kids.

Each child can be responsible for one small thing in the classroom. It might be clock monitor, bell monitor, lunch monitor or whatever. There are endless tasks that can be assigned to kids in any class to help satisfy their need for contribution.

Code words for contribution are: giving, sharing, helping, supporting, guiding, teaching and making a difference.

Another thing that soon became very obvious to me in that first hectic year at Macorna Primary School was that different kids learn in different ways. That is, they have different learning styles. Over the years education has evolved from a very one dimensional lesson delivery involving the 'chalk and talk' style to a much more multi dimensional style.

Key Learning Modes

Let's go back to Miss Young's year nine maths class and have a closer look at seven students with seven different learning styles.

Firstly, let's meet Bree. Bree is a great student who learns easily when lessons and information are presented visually to her. She is a **visual** learner who prefers to learn using pictures and images to understand new concepts.

Then there is Meg who really struggles with visually presented material because she learns best by hearing. Meg is an **aural** learner, so she needs concepts explained to her using sound. Integrating music into Meg's lessons is also going to help her learn.

Marg is a **verbal** learner who enjoys learning using the linguistic skills of reading, speaking and writing. She is an active participant in class discussions and enjoys oral presentations.

Tom of course is a **physical** learner who enjoys the kinesthetic, 'hands on' learning activities using active movement involving his body, hands and sense of touch.

Tran is a clear thinking, **logical** learner who prefers using logic, reasoning and systems when he learns. He can solve the Rubik's cube in no time but when it comes to creative activities like creative writing, he struggles.

Alli is the social butterfly of the class. She is universally popular with the girls and the boys and she learns best using **social** activities where she can learn collaboratively in groups or with a partner.

Ben is the opposite to Alli. He enjoys keeping to himself and can be described as a **solitary** learner who works alone and studies by himself.

One of the great advantages teachers of the 21st century like Miss Young have over their predecessors is the ability to cater for kids with all sorts of learning preferences using modern technology. 'Text book teaching' and 'chalk and talk' lesson delivery can much more easily be replaced with learning activities students can choose to match their preferred learning styles. Some text books now contain links to video tutorials which students can watch and listen to alone or in groups depending on their learning preferences. Youtube offers video learning tutorials for all types of school learning and it is now quite easy for teachers to video lessons so that students have support with homework and assignments.

But there is much more to understanding and teaching kids than just meeting their six needs and catering for their learning styles.

Understanding a child's brain development is essential knowledge for teachers in the 21st century. Let me be blunt. Teachers (and parents) must keep in mind that kids do not have an adult brain and they will not until they are in their early to mid twenties. 'Old' thinking taught us that human brains were pretty much fully developed by age 14 but MRI (magnetic resonance imaging) technology has shown us different. Now we know that adolescent brains are undergoing a major reconstruction that will not be completed until they are in their twenties. Now we know that the right and left sides of girls brains are 30% more connected than boys brains. Do schools take account of this?

Sometimes I wonder.

If I walked into Miss Young's year nine maths class before her lesson begins, this is what I would expect to see:

- the majority of the boys will be glued to their ipad/netbook playing computer games
- the majority of the girls will be sitting around chatting to each other.

How should we read this situation? Simple. Boys think, act, behave and learn differently to girls. To state the obvious, they are different than girls physically, mentally, socially and emotionally. So why don't we cater for these differences in our classrooms and our schools?

Don't worry; I know how difficult it is for a male teacher to understand what it is like to be a girl but we should at least try to understand how girls operate and to cater for them in our lesson planning. On the other hand, female teachers like Miss Young will benefit from learning some key strategies for working with boys like Tom and understanding how they operate.

Let's have a look at what Miss Young can do with a boy like Tom:

- Use a teacher directed learning style with very clear expectations to complete a set amount of work each lesson will be a good start with Tom. Most boys do not respond well to unstructured learning in open plan classrooms.
- Negotiate two fair and consistent rules that Tom (and the rest of the class) must meet. The first rule might be that Tom must complete his set work task satisfactorily in class time each lesson. The second rule might be that Tom does not behave in a way that distracts other students from their work. Two rules are enough for most boys and they need to be clear, consistently applied across the whole class and supported by agreed consequences if not adhered to.

- Loose boundaries and inconsistent consequences are an issue especially in secondary schools where students like Tom might have nine or ten different teachers. Tom will require a school wide plan where all teachers follow his Individual Learning Plan consistently. Structure, routine and consistency are great for boys.
- Boys like Tom respond well to active learning so Miss Young might alternate passive activities which last for no longer than 20 minutes with active ones.
- Nothing will motivate Tom more than a little bit of success so it is important that Miss Young gives Tom some success and then gradually build on it. As psychologist Andrew Fuller says, "Once a boy believes he can be successful, he'll almost always live up to it."
- Boys hate being embarrassed in front of their classmates so a struggler like Tom will feel embarrassed if forced to read aloud. Miss Young would be well advised to always give Tom the choice about reading out loud in front of his class.

Tom loves playing computer games. Have you ever stopped to wonder why computer games are so attractive to boys? It is simply because computer games tick a lot of boxes for them, for example:

- they challenge them (need for uncertainty).
- they are sequential and broken up into ascending stages (need for certainty).
- they get success by being challenged at every level until they succeed (need for significance).
- they learn by doing. Computer games are highly interactive which suits a boy's learning style of doing, then thinking, then talking (need for growth).
- they are competitive and turn boys into heroes. Boys (and men for that matter) aspire to being heroes. (need for significance).
- they can be played with partners or teams against partners and teams (need for connection).

Computer games show us how to teach boys. Challenge them using a sequential format where they experience success in an active and competitive learning environment where there is a possibility for connection with others, and you can't go wrong. 'Gamification' is a new educational tool where games are created as learning activities.

So what works for girls?

Girls respond best:

- if they know their teachers like them. They are very adept at reading negative body language so teachers who display positive body language will generally find girls respond well to them.
- if they feel like they fit in well and can succeed. Helping girls feel like they are an important part of the class and acknowledging their contributions will be well worth the effort.
- if given responsibilities and timeframes.
- with concrete learning activities. Abstract concepts can confuse and frustrate girls so try to improve skills like their spatial abilities through hands-on activities.
- if they can be self reliant. By all means help them, but then get out of their way and let them continue.
- when men (read male teachers) simply listen to their problems. Now, being a male, I understand how good we feel when we are solving problems for women, but sometimes, all a girl wants is for a man to listen to her problems.

Let's sum up what Miss Young has learned about kids:

- Kids learn best when they are interested in what they are learning.
- The six basic personality needs are: certainty, uncertainty, connection, significance, growth and contribution.
- The key learning modes are: visual, aural, verbal, physical, logical, solitary and social.
- Boys and girls learn differently.

Chapter 2 Resources:

1. Strategic Intervention Coach Training. Robbins-Madanes Center for Strategic Management

2. www.andrewfuller.com.au

Chapter Three

The Three Legged Stool

> "If the family isn't concerned about their son or daughter's education, it makes it very, very difficult for us teachers. If the parent thinks education is important, that student is really easy to teach."
>
> **(Trevor Hunt, secondary school teacher)**

Chapter Three

The Three Legged Stool

Warning: This chapter may be confrontational to some. It contains a blunt assessment of how it really is in our homes and our schools. It might be a good time to 'empty the glass' of all your thoughts and ideals and refill it slowly as you read through this section.

Miss Young's year nine maths class consisted of 24 students. If we apply nation wide statistical averages to this group we will find: at least one of the girls will have already been sexually abused; at least two of the students have already witnessed family violence; at least two students will be diagnosed with ADHD (Attention Deficit Hyperactive Disorder); at least eight students will drink alcohol on a weekly basis; at least eight students will not eat breakfast before school; at least six students will live in a one parent family. This unfortunate perspective of Miss Young's class is repeated across classrooms all over Australia and gives us an up-to-date view of the underlying causes of some of the issues today's students contend with at home and consequently bring to school.

An important element forming the foundation of any child's education is the three way relationship between their school, their teachers and their parents. We can compare this relationship with a three legged stool where one leg represents the school, the second leg represents the teachers and the third leg represents the parents. The child's education sits on that stool and if any one of those legs fails for whatever reason, the stool collapses and so does the child's education.

For instance:

- when **schools** fail to communicate effectively with parents through things like newsletters, parent-teacher interviews, and school reports, parents can easily start to feel isolated and disowned from their child's education

- when **teachers** do not effectively communicate to parents with issues like parent-teacher interviews, behavioural issues or the day to day issues that arise with students, parents start to feel that the teacher is not supporting their child effectively
- when **parents** do not ensure their child attends school or they are giving their child negative messages about their education, they put their own child's education at risk

An important part of any school's role is to nurture and support this three way relationship with its parent body and teacher body on behalf of the students. A good deal of this role inevitably falls on the teacher's shoulders with responsibilities, keeping parents informed about their child's academic progress and a host of other school related issues such as homework, excursions, class rules and breaches of behaviour standards.

On the other hand, schools have the responsibility for engaging and encouraging the parent body to support their child at school with things like:

- providing a healthy breakfast, snacks and lunches so that their child's nutritional program is at an optimum level to support the brain
- ensuring parents are well informed about their child's homework and assessment obligations
- keeping their child in a positive frame of mind about school attendance and the opportunity education offers them
- purchasing the books and equipment the child requires for their classes so that the child has all the resources they will need to progress academically and participate effectively in school programs
- attending parent-teacher interviews so that both teacher and student know that the parents are interested in, and supportive of, the student's progress
- having a general expectation that their child 'toes the line' at school and supports the various school policies on uniform, hair, mobile phones and such.

One of the things that has changed over the years is that schools now take a much stronger lead in driving the roles, expectations and responsibilities of parents. As well, 'Big Brother', in the form of government, now threatens parents with financial and legal threats if they do not meet community expectations for things like having their children vaccinated and school truancy.

Another change is the increase of families where both parents work, or there is only one parent. Consequently, we don't seem to see the same level of parent involvement in schools these days as when I attended school.

Successful schools have taken parent involvement very seriously ever since education began in Australia back in the gold rush days during the latter half of the 19th century. Schools back then were initiated by parents and communities who got together and lobbied government for a school. That is exactly what happened in 1872 when Concongella Primary School No 1136 came into existence and my great grandmother was one of the first students enrolled. Parents conceived this school and parents have always had an active part in the running of the school. Since my great grandmother's days this small rural school in North Western Victoria has enjoyed the help and support of five generations of my family as well as the vast majority of other district families who've had kids attend the school. They have run the school committee (now school council), the Mother's Club, the annual school sports, the transport to the swimming program, the working bees, the Christmas breakup, the monthly dances and all sorts of incidental activities to benefit the kids.

This little school is one of the lucky ones that still largely enjoys and encourages parent involvement today, but even its level of participation is changing because parents are no longer encouraged to be involved with swimming programs; no longer are the District School Sports run by a parent body; no longer does the Concongella Mother's Club exist.

Somewhere around the turn of this century the Ministry of Education decided to take control of the finances of the Concongella Mother's Club. That meant all funds raised by the Mother's Club were to come under the umbrella of the school finances which the department controlled and scrutinised. The Mother's

Club effectively lost control of the funds they were raising and where they could be spent. For 125 years the Concongella Mother's Club had raised funds locally and spent them on projects they devised for the benefit of the kids. Playground equipment was purchased, complete sets of readers were installed in the school library, sporting equipment was donated and all sorts of activities and excursions were funded through the Mother's Club. It was a club that was run from grassroots community support, not just from the mothers involved with the school but from grandmothers, friends and relatives. Over the years they made an enormous contribution to our school.

The moment government got involved using the grounds of financial accountability, the Mother's Club withered and died and along with it went a lot of community support and goodwill. This was never a decision for the benefit of the kids. It was a 'top down' decision for the benefit of the administration and it has seriously undermined the parent and community involvement in the school. This top down, 'we know better than you' attitude on the grounds of financial accountability is decimating community organisations which used to run beautifully on local volunteer support. This type of policy has also infiltrated a number of other local community organisations including the local Country Fire Authority Brigade which has disappeared under the threat of 'Big Brother' thinking.

But let's get back to the parent's role at supporting their child at school. If we take a quick look over the students in Miss Young's year nine maths class we will see a range of students being affected by home issues. So now we come to…

10 Quick And Easy Short Cuts For Ruining The Education Of Any School Child

Short Cut 1.

Feed them junk food and even better than that, send them off to school without breakfast or a half decent school lunch. Providing poor nutrition is a great way to propel children into all sorts of behavioural and learning problems at school.

An estimated 32% of students do not eat breakfast before going to school and "we already know that kids' concentration and ability to learn is worse when they miss breakfast." (Dr Gavin Sandercock from the University of Essex). An English study conducted by Dr Sandercock also found that "girls who skipped breakfast are 92% more likely to become obese than female classmates who regularly eat before school; the equivalent figure in boys was 62%. But the boys were much likelier than female classmates to have a sedentary lifestyle and, critically, have poor cardiorespiratory (heart and lung) fitness."

Antidotes:

- Feed kids a healthy breakfast every day including school days.
- In his book, 'Good News For The Alphabet Kids', Dr Michael Sichel explains just how vital nutrition is to a child's wellbeing. I recommend this book as it contains a complete nutritional guide for children plus a step-by-step menu plan with a large range of healthy recipes.
- For schools this means providing healthy food alternatives at school canteens using fresh ingredients. Providing quality lunches made using quality ingredients enables the kids to taste the difference, which in turn encourages healthy eating habits.
- There are times when teachers use food for rewards or for special occasions. These occasions are opportunities to support the healthy eating ethos so that the kids in class develop an awareness of healthy alternatives and the benefits for their health when they make the choice for healthy foods.
- Whole school, consistent education messages around healthy eating should be employed.

Short Cut 2.

Lie to them. That way they won't trust anyone and they will learn how to deceive everyone else, including themselves, with lies, excuses and half truths. This will help them to not take themselves or their school work seriously and to make excuses as to why they can't keep up in class or with homework.

Deceit is an insidious tool to use against kids. Yes, we all use it at times with things like Santa and Easter Bunny and I'm not suggesting we give away the Tooth Fairy.

What I'm talking about is telling Billy he can have free time after he has cleaned his room and then going back on your word, or promising to take the kids to the movies and then making excuses not to go because it doesn't suit you. Being open and honest with kids builds a foundation of trust and understanding that will stand parents in good stead when they get to the tricky adolescent years.

Antidotes:

- Own up when you make a mistake. Covering up mistakes by deceit and lying is a very quick way of losing your child's trust and teaches them to do the same.
- Be true to your word. If you offer your child a reward when they accomplish something, be a great role model and live up to your promise.
- Acknowledge your kids when you see them acting with integrity and honesty.
- Role play situations involving honesty. For example, you are working after school at the local newsagent when a lady pays for a $6.50 purchase with two ten dollar notes stuck together. What should you do?

  A. Put both ten dollar notes in the till and hand back $3.50 in change

  B. Hand one ten dollar note back to the customer plus the change

  C. Put one ten dollar note in your pocket and hand back $3.50 in change

Short Cut 3.

Act poorly in front of them. As their role model, teach them how to use violence and rage, throw hissy fits, make excuses for themselves, run everyone down, blame others and generally feel good about treating their teachers and other kids with disrespect.

Kids subconsciously copy and learn from the adults around them from a very young age. My two little grandkids have been copying adult behaviour since before they were 12 months old and they don't separate good behaviour to copy from bad. It can be very embarrassing when your four year old parrots something you have said privately about someone, to their face... "Mum said you ..."

Antidotes:

- If parents display good manners, respect for others and a friendly personality, then there is a good chance their kids will follow suit. Kids learn so much from copying parents so give them positive behaviour to copy. This is far more effective than talking to them.
- Show your kids how to follow the rules. I hate it when I see parents walk against the red lights with their kids in tow. Can we please educate our kids to use the roads safely and responsibly? It would be a great start to improving our driving behaviour and it may save some kids being hit by cars as pedestrians.
- Kids at school like to impress their peers by using bad language, being cheeky and acting poorly. Parents and schools need to send a consistent message to students that there is a time and place for letting our language slip and for 'acting the goat', but at school and inside the classroom is not one of those times.
- Teachers also are seriously important role models for their students. This doesn't mean that teachers need to be perfect. It means that teachers try to be open and honest when they make a mistake and it means that teachers are true to their own rules. If it is good enough for

kids to put money in the fine jar when they let poor language slip, then it is good enough for teachers to do the same.

Short Cut 4.

Allow your kids to rule. Don't burden them with rules, expectations or responsibility for actions; just let them do as they please whenever they please including at home and at school. And while you're at it, let them experiment with sex, drugs, alcohol and smoking from a young age. It's all part of their education, right?

Kids need to have boundaries and it is a parent's job to set the boundaries at home. I know it is unrealistic for me to expect all parents to set clear and consistent boundaries for their kids, but for parents who want to make a difference, consider the following antidotes.

Antidotes:

- Discuss with your kids some house rules which set the behavioural and language standards in the home.
- Come up with some clear boundaries for computer use for your kids. For example, no computers in bedrooms or after 9pm.
- Negotiate some simple boundaries for mobile phone use. For example, mobile phones go on the charging table at 9pm each night until 8am the next morning.
- Agree on curfews appropriate to age where kids must be home by this time and in bed by that time.
- Educate your kids to 'operate above the magic line' by helping them to take ownership of their problems, accept responsibility for their actions and be responsible for fixing their mistakes.

Short Cut 5.

Show your kids how to be a slob. Inspire them not to exercise. Allow them to laze around amongst their unkempt belongings and not help out in the home. Don't ever ask them about getting their homework done on time and laugh with them when they forget to take their Phys Ed uniform to school or decide to wag school whenever it suits them. Help them to treat school as a joke and to only go when it suits them.

There is an old saying that "if you give a kid an inch, they will take a mile". It is important that parents understand this and how it can impact on their child's education.

Antidotes:

- Support the school with homework expectations by ensuring they make time for it and have a quiet space to complete homework.
- Take responsibility for your child's attendance at school. "Every day missed in school is a lost social and educational opportunity that cannot be reclaimed. It increases the child's position of disadvantage." (Mypolonga Primary School & Community Newsletter)
- You pay for your child's books and uniforms and school equipment so you have every right to expect they value them, take pride in them and look after them.
- Ensure your child takes responsibility for contributing around their home and for their own welfare with things like healthy eating, keeping active and being tidy.

Short Cut 6.

Employ violence to control your family or embrace a dysfunctional family life with a parade of alternative partners so that they learn that relationships are really shallow emotional events to get what you want when you want. Teach them that using the other sex for their own gain is quite acceptable at school and turn a blind eye when they bully other kids like you bully them.

Family violence statistics reveal that 33.3% of women had experienced physical violence since the age of 15 and "the 2012 Personal Safety Survey found that 54 per cent of women who had experienced violence by a current partner had children in their care at the time and 31 per cent said that children had witnessed the violence." (http://www.aph.gov.au) These statistics confirm that many school age children are exposed to family violence. Sexual abuse statistics reveal that 12.4% of women had been sexually abused **before** the age of 15. (http://www.domesticviolence.com.au)

Antidotes:

- All parents get into tiffs and arguments from time to time. A joint agreement that any disagreements or issues get sorted through away from the children will help shield them from the damage that comes from seeing their parents having a white hot argument or physically abusing each other. It really is a policy of 'it's all about the kids'.
- Help your kids talk to someone they trust about any emotional issues that come up for them. It may well be the school psychologist or wellbeing coordinator, a teacher they champion or a grandparent, but talking about the issues will help them.
- Get help from Community Care organisations such as Helpline, Beyond Blue, Kids Helpline or online help at http://www.whiteribbon.org.au/finding-help.

Short Cut 7.

Tune out and ignore them. Don't listen to them, ignore their problems at school and take absolutely no interest in them at all because life is all about 'me'. I'm too tired, I don't understand it and I'm really just not interested. I hated school so why should you enjoy it?

There's nothing more demoralizing for a child than to be shunned and ignored by their parents. And yet, all too often the frenetic pace of everyday life lures parents into forgetting the simple things like giving their children attention. It is a demoralizing problem that is so simple to overcome.

Antidotes:

- Give them your attention and show them you care. "The best inheritance a parent can give to his children is a few minutes of their time each day." (M. Grundler)
- Kids of both sexes crave adult attention because it helps meet their need for significance. Simply encourage your kids to get involved in the things you do (even if it is just helping you cook dinner) and they will feel as though they are a valuable part of your family. You will help prevent them seeking adult attention in ways that put them at risk.
- Have designated one-on-one time for each child with each parent. For example, each parent spends time one-on-one with each child every week. You might read together, watch a movie together, play a board game together; it doesn't matter what it is. What matters is they get your undivided attention. You might be surprised what comes out in the conversation when you do this simple activity with your kids.
- The old fashioned idea of going for a Sunday afternoon drive is well worth considering. You have a captive audience in the car for all sorts of fun activities and you get to decide where your next driving adventure might take you. Or even better, let your kids decide where to go every so often.

Short Cut 8.

Bag out their teachers and school, especially when they are in hearing range. It will make you feel really important to bring their teachers and their school back a peg or two and it will encourage your child to treat their school, their teachers, you and themselves with the disrespect that you use to empower yourself.

Parents have an important role in supporting a positive mindset about school with their kids. While it might be tempting to unleash your wrath and frustration with teachers and school in earshot of your children, you are doing them and their education a great disservice. Do you really want to encourage your kids to hate school?

Antidotes:

- When problems occur at school, instead of bagging out their teacher, go and sit down with the teacher and have a chat about how you can both work together to solve the problem. It is in the interests of both the parent and the teacher to find solutions which will benefit the child. If you get stuck for solutions, try asking the child.
- One of the most powerful things a parent can do with their school kid is to sit down with them every night and get them to teach the parent what they have learnt today. It will only take 5 minutes and it will help your child revise what they have just learnt. It will also help parents keep track of what their kids are learning at school.
- We parents are salesmen for the benefits of education for the future happiness of our kids and the reality is, "if we are not better salesmen than the drug salesman down at the end of the street, our kids lose." (Darren Stephens, Global Publishing Group) So sell the virtues of education to your kids and help them understand that all the negative messages about school they are exposed to on social media and YouTube will not benefit them, nor will turning to drugs and alcohol for relief.

Short Cut 9.

Give them money for nothing. Teach them how to access and max out a credit card, how to let every cent they get slip through their fingers, how to expect money for nothing and how to suck every dollar they can from government agencies, Centrelink, their school and anybody else they come in contact with.

Antidotes:

- Leave money in the house in full view of kids. That way kids will learn that having money sitting around does not mean that it is theirs for the taking.
- Involve kids in family finance decisions. We need to be careful to not burden or shame them but involving kids in discussions about family finances helps educate and empower them for when their turn comes.
- Teach kids to earn their own money, including pocket money and how to look after it.
- Teach kids to be financially independent by living within their means. Loaning money to them to buy the next new shiny object is a great way of teaching kids to live outside their means.
- Scott Pape has some excellent strategies for teaching kids about money. I recommend his book 'The Barefoot Investor' and his investment strategies.

Short Cut 10.

Tell them that they are useless, good for nothing cretins. Run them down at every opportunity, tell them that you don't love them and didn't want them in the first place, and make a point of comparing them unfavourably to their brothers and sisters.

It is a regular part of my role as a tutor and a coach to counsel kids who come to me with stories about having received one of the above messages from a parent, family member or a teacher. Putting disparaging labels on kids will affect their self identity and help them truly believe they are useless, bad, unlovable or whatever. When they take these labels on board and believe they are true, they will act out the reality they believe. All kids have times when their behaviour needs correcting but labeling them as bad kids or useless or evil or lazy will never help them.

Antidotes:

- We can correct poor behaviour, not by labeling kids, but by talking to them about their poor behaviour. For example, "Bill, I was disappointed to see you behaving so cruelly with the cat. C'mon, you know better than that." Instead of, "Bill you are a cruel, sadistic boy."
- We can praise kids when they do well and support them when they struggle or fail through encouragement and praise for effort. For example, "I know you didn't get the result you were looking for Abe but I was really impressed with the effort you put in. Keep it up."
- We can empower our kids to be responsible by giving them some things to be responsible for. For example, make our kids responsible for keeping their rooms tidy. That gives us plenty of opportunity to praise them when they make the bed well, put their dirty clothes in the laundry, pack up their toys, or whatever.
- We can understand that all kids are unique and different to each other. Comparing them only sets up poor harmony between the two kids. Help your kids understand that they are not clones of their brothers and sisters and therefore will bring their own unique mix of abilities and disabilities to the table.

That's it! That's ten simple, easy ways for parents to create a completely dysfunctional kid who will go through life feeling sorry for themselves, treating others poorly, and with no purpose, no motivation and no tools or strategies to create success for themselves.

Sorry! I needed to get that off my chest and I accept that there are still many students who come from loving homes where mum and dad do care and take an active involvement in their child's education. But the harsh reality is that teachers today are working with some kids that come out of families where those ten short cuts are a fact of life. They result in students developing unhealthy and disempowering habits and mindsets which they bring into classrooms and as a result put even more pressure on teachers.

So to finish off, here is a summary of my ten most powerful tactics for parents to support their child at school:

1. **Do** teach them the benefits of healthy eating.
2. **Do** be honest and own up to your mistakes.
3. **Do** be a positive role model.
4. **Do** negotiate clear boundaries.
5. **Do** teach them how to be responsible for themselves.
6. **Do** protect your child from violence in your home.
7. **Do** spend a few minutes of your time with your kids every day.
8. **Do** sell the benefits of education.
9. **Do** teach financial literacy through example.
10. **Do** resist putting negative labels on kids.

Chapter 3 Resources:

1. Recommended reading:
   'Good News For The Alphabet Kids' (Dr Michael Sichel)
   'The Barefoot Investor' (Scott Pape)

2. www.theguardian.com/society/2010/aug/16/third-pupils-skip-breakfast

3. http://www.aph.gov.au and http://www.domesticviolence.com.au

4. Community Care organisations such as Helpline, Beyond Blue, Kids Helpline or online help at http://www.whiteribbon.org.au/finding-help

5. Aussie Kids Coach presentation:
   10 Quick And Easy Short Cuts For Ruining The Education Of Any School Child

   Further details from: www.DynamicTeachingTools.com

Chapter Four

Drawing The Battle Lines

> *"Every child deserves a champion, an adult who will not give up on them, who understands the power of connection and insists they become the best that they can possibly be."*
>
> **(Rita Pierson TED Talk)**

Chapter Four

Drawing The Battle Lines

One of the big issues Miss Young is having in her year nine maths class is keeping her students on task. We've seen Tom with the wanders, kids playing games on ipads, others without text books and others being upset by students distracting them. Classroom management tools are a crucial part of any teacher's tool kit because without a well run classroom, students simply cannot learn effectively. As we have seen, providing a safe, secure classroom learning environment which caters for kids needs is essential especially when we have 21st century kids bringing all sorts of outside issues into the classroom.

If Ben has been listening to mum and dad arguing all night, there's a good chance he will not be at his best in class the next day.

If Meg has come to school without breakfast and with chips and a muesli bar for lunch at best, don't be surprised if she can't think straight in the latter part of the school day.

If Syd had his ipad confiscated for the day in period one, his subsequent classes will be difficult because he'll not be able to complete work on his ipad and he'll not be able do research, use his e-texts or access his work for some subjects from Google Classroom.

If Izzy is quiet and withdrawn today because she's been on the receiving end of some nasty social media exchanges with her friends, don't be surprised if she doesn't switch on in class.

If Jack and Josh have just had a 'barney' in the school yard things might just be a bit tense between them in the classroom. The adrenalin will still be running and getting angry again will only be a touch away.

Teachers have to be ready for these types of issues with their students every day and in every class. We also shouldn't forget that teachers are human too and they

have days when they feel a bit off. They have days when they are worried by home issues and they have days when something at school has upset them. As we saw in Chapter One, a teacher's mindset is critical if they are to teach effectively despite what might be going on for them outside the classroom.

But mindset is only one part of effective teaching. If teachers don't have the tools and strategies to keep their classes well managed, the flow on effect is a poor learning environment in the classroom, poor student engagement and a lack of student learning. A teacher's classroom management skills are the foundation that all great teachers construct student learning around. I could easily write a whole book just on classroom management so I've had to keep this chapter brief and to the point.

So let's send Miss Young off to a professional development course to improve her classroom management skills. The course was called....

The 8 Step Plan To Cultivate Outstanding Classroom Management

Cultivating Classroom Management Step 1: Developing rapport

Developing rapport is all about building a trusting working relationship with students that supports effective learning. It is not about becoming friends with students. It is about creating a friendly working relationship so that students feel safe and secure, challenged and excited, connected with classmates, significant, contributing and growing academically. Building rapport with students was a foundation teaching skill which was clearly overlooked in Miss Young's teacher training. However, she soon learnt that simple tools can have a powerful impact on students, that 'small hinges swing big doors'. She learnt things like how to:

- use a warm, firm handshake as a powerful rapport building tool
- smile – it is worth a thousand words
- have fun in class and use laughter therapy as a great rapport building tool

- use eye contact (if culturally appropriate) to help students know you value them
- use subtle mimicking of student body language
- ask open questions of students to encourage effective communication
- practice active listening
- see things from a student's perspective and don't be judgemental
- match a student's language patterns and words rather than using edubabble (technical language that schools use)
- copy the student's voice tone, speed and volume to help them feel comfortable and understood
- dress to impress students of both sex
- use positive body language.

"Once teachers have developed strong working relationships and a sense of trust and understanding with students, they will 'gift' the teacher the authority to teach them."

(Ian Davies)

Miss Young also learned the key things to avoid when building rapport, such as avoid:

- being judgemental and labelling students as bad or lazy
- acting insincerely, using off hand remarks and false praise
- ignoring and starving even the most trying kids of attention
- using sarcasm as a weapon
- being trivial about student concerns
- being aggressive and using persistent confrontation of students
- being dishonest with students and not owning up when you make a mistake

"Kids don't remember what you try to teach them.
They remember what you are."

(Jim Henson)

Cultivating Classroom Management Step 2: Rules, rights and more rules

Miss Young soon learned that the second key to cultivating successful classroom management is to develop student ownership of the rules and rights that students have in her classroom.

She learnt how to:

- establish workable rules which set boundaries for student behaviour; clear, concise rules that everyone understands; rules that are taught, and reinforced constantly; rules that students have ownership of by constructing the rules themselves (with guidance); rules that are easy to obey. A big trap for teachers is to develop so many rules that it is impossible to monitor and enforce them.
- model good student and teacher behaviour so that it becomes the entrenched norm in everyday classroom practices
- teach student rights in her classroom; understand others rights; encourage the right to express opinions and needs; facilitate and value each child's right to be an individual; promote self-paced learning; ensure students have access to teacher help when required; manage the right to a drink/toilet break; provide for each child's right to be involved class activities
- establish rules that have clear consequences and are firmly, fairly and consistently applied. For example, a very successful teacher that we will meet later in this book has a very successful little saying when students call out in class. He simply says, "I love your enthusiasm, but hate your manners." So he doesn't have a rule for answering questions, but he has an expectation and he reinforces it constantly and consistently across the class. Even the kids now parrot that saying when they know they have made a mistake and called out.
- provide for each student's right and expectation to learn through creating a well managed classroom where structured learning activities helped students see their academic progress.

As a general rule, schools and teachers over-complicate education with far too many rules. For teenage boys, two to three rules are all they can handle. Does this mean we let teenage boys run riot? Absolutely not! Constant messages and expectations can replace many rules as long as students feel they have ownership of the decision making process.

Cultivating Classroom Management Step 3: Discipline

Teachers can no longer demand respect through authoritarian means. Teachers today have to earn the respect of students.

Back in 'the good old days' many teachers ruled their classrooms with an iron fist loaded with classroom management tools like the strap, physical intimidation, embarrassment, the dunce's hat, the naughty corner and even ear twisting and hair pulling. These old days are gone and in my experience it is just as well. I had the unpleasant experience many years ago of resorting to the blackboard ruler for discipline and it resulted in a sharp deterioration in the classroom learning environment and a complete loss of rapport with my students and their parents. A big mistake on my part but a lesson well learned.

Fast forward to 2015 and Miss Young's professional development program in classroom management taught her how to discipline students 21st century style.

The first unit of discipline training is aimed at creating student self discipline and a sense of ownership, accountability and responsibility for behaviour.

It taught Miss Young how to:

- encourage self control
- develop positive attitudes towards things like honesty, manners and respect
- enhance social skills such as tolerance of others, leadership and just getting along
- promote self motivation and purpose
- help students take responsibility for their academic progress and behavior.

The second unit of discipline training taught Miss Young the three spheres of classroom discipline:

1. Proactive discipline. Proactive discipline strategies are intended to prevent behavioural issues before they happen. They include:

    - students knowing and understanding the rules. It may also involve students having an active part in setting the rules
    - students being familiar with the step-by-step school discipline policy. For example, warning - lunch detention - after school detention – suspension
    - keeping the classroom clean, well organised and even attractive
    - students receiving clear expectations about work quality and quantity
    - keeping all class equipment in good working order, especially the multi media equipment. There is nothing more frustrating for students and teacher alike when the video player won't work or the internet connection is lost
    - ensuring students of all abilities are catered for in the lesson content
    - students role playing potential behavioural issues and solutions

2. On the spot discipline, which includes strategies such as:

    - verbal corrections when students are disruptive or off task
    - tactical ignoring of some attention seeking behaviour
    - 'time out' of the classroom
    - correction signs or signals
    - questioning potential behavioural issues
    - allowing students to choose their next course of action
    - changing the seating arrangement
    - revisiting class or school rules

3. Follow up discipline tools, such as:

    - catching up with students after class, in private
    - teacher managed discipline where teachers decide the best way to discipline the child
    - peer managed discipline where trained students negotiate consequences with the student being disciplined
    - counseling by School Wellbeing Coordinator, House Leaders, Leadership Team
    - negotiating Student Behaviour Contracts
    - talking to parents about student behaviour

Cultivating Classroom Management Step 4: Be prepared

The old scout motto 'Be Prepared' was instilled in me right through my time as a cub and as a boy scout. The benefits of being prepared were not just hammered into us as far as being physically prepared but more importantly for being mentally prepared. We have already spoken at length about mental preparation and mindset in Chapter One so now we move on to being prepared for the battle of classroom management. Being prepared is really a common sense way of approaching life but there are teachers out there who choose to walk out of the staffroom door with little more than a text book and a whiteboard marker as their preparation.

Miss Young was diligent at planning her class activities but that doesn't mean she was well prepared for the ongoing classroom behaviour battles. Being prepared means Miss Young knew in her own mind which strategy she was going to pull out of her coat of many pockets when Tom started distracting other students or when Beth used her mobile phone again.

The Be Prepared unit of her profession development showed Miss Young how to support her classroom management and minimize poor behaviour through:

    - improving student engagement using strategies which create surprise, curiosity, suspense, challenge, and along the way, meet the six basic personality needs

- developing a plan of what to do if…. If teachers already know what they are going to do, they will act decisively and quickly to prevent minor issues from developing into major barriers to learning
- using the power of choice to let students find their own learning level and match their preferred learning style
- educating the students to come to class with all the materials and books they require through a short term reward program using 'class money' that students accumulated and then cashed in for real rewards each month
- keeping a file of student agreements and contracts so that each child could be kept accountable for their agreements on the spot if needed
- being prepared for the inevitable technology breakdowns which can leave a well planned lesson high and dry. What do you do when the remote for the electronic whiteboard goes missing? Well, you have a back up plan just for that eventuality.

Cultivating Classroom Management Step 5: Positivity

The start of any lesson is crucial for teachers to set up their lesson well and put students in a positive learning state of mind. The last thing a secondary school teacher needs is to turn up to class five minutes late to find most of the boys playing games on their school ipad and most of the girls have gone into social chit-chat mode. When teachers are late for class, other students will drop off their books off and disappear for a quick drink or a quick toilet stop.

When this happens it is then a major task for teachers to bring the class together and then shift the student's state of mind back to the classroom learning intention. Helping students change state is an important skill for teachers like Miss Young. It helps students to leave their home and playground problems outside.

In this unit on Positive State of Mind, Miss Young learned how to strategically develop a positive student mindset and thus give herself and her students the best possible chance of learning.

She learnt how to:

- reframe an unruly start to a lesson by taking the whole class outside, lining them up, settling them down and giving them instructions as to what they do when they are instructed to re enter the classroom. For example, "Your first job is to …" A reminder of agreed class rules might also help
- use her own positive body language to show students that she is in charge and is confident at controlling a class full of diverse students
- create a well organised and attractive classroom environment that supports student learning. In my first year out of Teacher's College a teacher in a neighbouring school was brilliant at using her classroom to create positivity and she did it with the kids help. Together they transformed their classroom into an underwater world, Aladdin's cave and a witch's hideout as they studied successive themes. This created a 'state change' for the kids the moment they walked into the classroom and set them up for the next learning experience
- create special events which rewarded the class for their positive learning and behaviour. For example, during the summer you might put on a watermelon afternoon tea or a soup and toast morning tea during winter. There are lots of different ways teachers can encourage kids to be positive using special events
- build self esteem and a positive outlook. Little sayings such as, "Give it a go" and "You can do it" become part of the child's identity if done with encouragement and sincerity
- refocus the class when changing to a new activity or when things were not going so well. A sample of the refocus tools Miss Young learned to use were music anchors, special sounds such as a train whistle, physical signals, visual signs and interactive countdowns.

Cultivating Classroom Management Step 6: Reinforcement and reward

Miss Young is now well into her classroom management training and she has learned the basics of operating a highly functional classroom which not

only meets student needs, but develops effective learning. The next layer of strategies and tools she is experiencing is all about negative and positive reinforcement of the student attitudes and academic progress she is aiming for.

Firstly, let's have a look at the negative reinforcement strategies her next unit of training taught her:

- Tactical ignoring. This is a strategy Bill Rogers describes in his book, 'You Know The Fair Rule' for issues like calling out in class. I'll let Bill take up the story. "The reinforcement we planned operated on the basic notion that limited, tactical ignoring as first step might provide those calling out with a chance to stop. Their off task behaviour would not give them what they wanted, attention." However, tactical ignoring can't go on forever. If the unwanted behaviour continues, we need try another strategy.
- Constant reinforcement of the rules. For example, if a student is calling out, we might say something like, "Love the enthusiasm, hate the manners" or we might simply ask that the rule be followed with something like, "Josh, please use our rule for speaking in class" or "Josh, please raise your hand when you want to speak thanks." If that doesn't work we go to the next level.
- A change of environment to bring about compliance. This can either mean asking Josh to sit quietly on his own or asking him to wait outside the door. Give him three or four minutes and then go out and ask him what's going on and why he is choosing to ignore the rules. We might then suggest he re enters the class when he has changed his mind and agrees to follow the rules.
- Removal from the room as a last resort. If Josh is totally non compliant, Miss Young may have no other option than to have him removed for the rest of the class and counselled by the Wellbeing Coordinator or a member of the school leadership group.

The second part of Miss Young's training on reinforcement and rewards showed her how to incorporate positive reinforcement strategies into her teaching. The aim of positive reinforcement is to satisfy the student's need for significance and attention while they are on task. If we can satisfy this need while they are on task, we can eliminate them satisfying this need through off task attention seeking behaviours like calling out, distracting others and going for a wander.

The strategies Miss Young learned for positive reinforcement included:

- finding every available opportunity to use tactical verbal reinforcement and encouragement. For example, a quick comment such as, "Great job today Tom" or "Thanks for trying so hard on this Danni" reinforces their positive attitude to their work and encourages them to repeat it next time
- how to use tokens. Many primary school teachers use stars, stamps, weekly awards and the like as positive reinforcement tools with students. But we rarely see them used in secondary school. Do they work? Absolutely! I have used a weekly 'payment' system with several of my tutoring students using fake Australian dollars and this opened up a raft of real world learning activities from budgeting, to investing to shopping and so on
- how to use special interest activities as rewards for goal achievement, work targets and improved behaviour. Even a system similar to the scout badge system would work extremely well in the secondary school system. We'll discuss this concept more in the next chapter
- how one school who used a money reward system with students used the system as a negative and a positive reward system. This school allowed students to save (accumulate) their money over their school life. Each month, the school held class auctions where students could bid for real rewards (DVDs, CDs, stationary items, colouring books etc) using 'their' money. But on the other hand, poor behaviour earned a 'fine' which had to be paid out of savings.

Cultivating Classroom Management Step 7: Consistent conflict resolution tools

Miss Young's class is like all other classes. There are times when conflict needs to be dealt with quickly, without hostility and fairly. A key plank in any conflict resolution strategy is for the participants to take ownership of the problem and the solution, to accept that they can learn from it, and to take responsibility for creating a fair outcome. Being well prepared with a collection of conflict resolution tools, strategies and options, makes life a lot easier for teachers when the inevitable dispute happens.

In this unit of Miss Young's classroom management training she learnt to not only deal with conflict on the spot, but to minimize conflict from occurring in the first place and then use conflict incidents as valuable learning experiences for the whole class going forward.

So let's have a look at what she learned in these three areas of conflict resolution:

1. Conflict minimization is a key attribute of successful teachers as they skillfully defuse incidents before they have a chance to develop into a full blown conflict incident. These teachers are usually highly effective classroom managers who keep very good self control and who are adept at applying their favourite conflict minimization tools and strategies, such as:

   • creating a safe and pleasant classroom environment where students are encouraged to leave all their frustrations from home and the playground outside the class door
   • using 'change of state' activities to ensure students are in the best possible state of mind for the upcoming learning activities
   • defusing in-class frustrations between other students using the agreed rules and respect for other's rights
   • using repartee to take the heat out of tense situations. Bill Rogers, in his book 'Know The Fair Rule', shows us some excellent examples of using

repartee. Student: "I hate you" Teacher: Thanks for the compliment, now get back to work thanks." Student: "Bullshit" Teacher: "Where?" Student: "You bastard" Teacher: "Yeah so's my dog."

- constantly reinforcing great student behaviour so that it becomes the expected norm.

2. On the spot conflict is often the result of student frustration for one reason or another. It might be because of not being able to do the work, lack of assistance, other students disrupting them, a teacher's comment or any one of a number of other issues. But suddenly the frustration will boil over and the student will become agitated or angry and an argument or physical tussle erupts.

When this occurs some useful strategies a teacher might use are:

- take a deep breath or two or even three, slow down and concentrate on maintaining self control and not getting frustrated, annoyed or angry. Think before you speak
- to not allow student baiting to suck them in to a fruitless power struggle. For example, a student who calls out "This is boring" can easily encourage other students to chip in with their version like "When am I ever going to need this". An adept teacher will take the wind out of their sails with, "Yeah it is a bit boring so let's get stuck into it so we can move on to something more interesting."
- focus on the student's behaviour, not them. For example, if a student is pestering another student a teacher can easily get sucked into a comment like, "Josh, stop being a nuisance" which labels him the person as a nuisance. A more focused comment would be, "Josh, your behaviour at the moment is annoying Danni. We need to talk."
- have a Plan B in place. Plan B might be to call in for some assistance from a nearby teacher or a House Leader before an incident gets completely out of hand or you feel you are losing your self control
- once the conflict is over and those involved have cooled off a bit, follow up with all involved so that they learn that there are consequences for

their actions and that future behaviour like that is not acceptable.

3.   Conflict incidents provide teachers with first hand learning experiences to teach students how to behave appropriately in difficult circumstances. When Miss Young is disciplining Tom for aggressive behaviour she is in fact teaching the rest of the class how to (or how not to) deal with people who might act aggressively towards them in the future. The students will learn how to implement conflict resolution strategies by watching Miss Young use them.

Miss Young learnt how to use:

- role play activities where students practice dealing with aggression (in this case but it could be all sorts of other conflict situations) in mock situations
- students to film conflict role plays so that participants could review their performance and give feedback to each other
- classroom discussions of real life conflict incidents to investigate ways to resolve conflict before it becomes violent.

Cultivating Classroom Management Step 8: The ROAR Learning System

The final step Miss Young learnt to cultivate effective classroom management was to learn the ROAR Learning System. This is my way of incorporating classroom management into academic progress. This is how it works:

Review

The first part of any of my lessons is to review what we previously learnt. Students learn best when teachers link 'a known' to 'the unknown'. So the review process involves going back over the previous learning intention before moving on to the next unknown learning. This has the advantage of picking up any students who missed the previous class, supporting any students who are a bit shaky on the learning and it is an opportunity to have some fun at the start of a lesson and get everyone engaged.

There are lots of ways of reviewing but here are my three favourites:

- teacher directed class discussion using the **Pose - Pounce - Pause - Bounce** questioning method. This works really well if we use a spinning wheel app called Decide Now. It allows us to create a Spinning Wheel with each student's name on it. Then the teacher **poses** a question, **pounces** on a student selected by the spinning wheel, **pauses** for the student to answer, and then **bounces** to the next question. It is a bit of fun and keeps kids engaged because they know the spinning wheel is making the decision who to question and they just never know when their name will come up.
- ask students to **'teach back'** what they have learnt to the class. They can do this to the full class or to a partner. The Spinning Wheel app might come in useful to decide who does the teaching back.
- select students to do a 30 second **impromptu talk** on one aspect of the last lesson. For example, if we have started learning how to calculate the circumference of a circle, one impromptu talk might be about the difference between radius and diameter, another about what circumference measures and another about the circumference formulas.

Ownership

The next part of my lesson is usually teacher directed but it doesn't have to be. It aims at ensuring students understand clearly the relevance of the next learning intention to them and the real world. It is really important for teachers to explain how their learning is relevant to them. If we can't do that then we should question why we are teaching the topic in the first place. This is a good opportunity to bring some variety into the classroom in the form of:

- props from the real world. For example, bring in an old tyre and explain that today's lesson will teach students how far a car will travel on one revolution of the tyre
- guest speakers to explain how they use circumference in their work

- a Youtube video explaining how circumference is applied in real life
- a practical demonstration of circumference at work.

Advance

We are now probably 15 minutes into the lesson and ready to advance on to the unknown, the new learning intention. We have already revised the knowledge we need to know, we have explained how the new learning can benefit the students, and now we are ready to learn the next piece. How do we do it?

Generally this sequence is followed:

- ask students to write down the learning intention
- ask students to write in their own words how this piece of learning will benefit them
- explain the next step, for example, work through an example of calculating circumference
- ask the students to record the calculation in their work book
- practice the skill using at least six practice problems
- focus some more on practical application of the skill.

Reflect

The final step in the ROAR Learning System is to reflect on what has been learnt by students and their teacher. Some ideas for achieving this step are:

- class discussion of what has been learnt
- an understanding scale. It might be thumbs up for good understanding, thumbs down for poor understanding, thumbs side ways for shaky understanding or a scaling mark out of 10
- a feedback sheet designed to measure how the student feels they learnt the topic
- group discussion of the learning to answer some given questions which measure how students feel they learnt the topic
- do a mock interview of several students to gauge how they feel they learnt the topic.

Part of the reflection should also seek feedback on how well the students feel their teacher taught the topic. It can be a bit daunting asking students how well you taught the topic but it will really help you improve if you know from the kids what has worked and what hasn't with which kids.

The ROAR Learning System is designed to stack learning one brick at a time and I have found it gives the students a lot of confidence and a positive outlook for each lesson.

The other thing about the ROAR Learning System is that it lends itself beautifully to the One hour - One day - One week Memory System. This system of aiding retention of learned skills works well. If a student revises a new skill one hour after they have learnt it (for example, at the completion of the lesson), and then revises it again the following day (for example, in another lesson or by 'teaching back' at home), and then revises it again one week later (for example, in next week's lesson), I have found a considerable improvement in skill retention.

Effective classroom management is a foundation skill every teacher needs to continually work on if their teaching is going to be effective for their students.

Chapter 4 Resources:

1. 'Cultivating Classroom Management' Professional Development Course for Teachers

   For further details: www.DynamicTeachingTools.com

2. The ROAR learning system www.DynamicTeachingTools.com

   Access to details of this learning system is provided free to all Dynamic Teaching Tools members at: www.DynamicTeachingTools.com

3. Recommended reading: 'You Know The Fair Rule' (Bill Rogers)

Chapter Five

The Hidden Curriculum

"Beliefs have the power to create and the power to destroy. Human beings have the awesome ability to take any experience from their lives and create a meaning that either disempowers them or one that literally saves their lives."
(Tony Robbins)

The Hidden Curriculum

In the first chapter, Miss Young learnt a lot about her mindset and how important it is to effective teaching. She also came to the realisation that if she could apply what she had learnt about mindset to her students, they would become better prepared for the challenges of not only school life, but adult life as well.

One of the key learnings that Miss Young took from her coaching sessions with Todd was that a person's mindset is the foundation for their success in life. She learnt that operating below the magic line was disempowering and that developing superior habits was something successful teachers had mastered. Miss Young now understood that while the academic curriculum was important, even more important was the 'hidden curriculum' where students learnt about themselves, about creating success, about effective communication and about learning from mistakes.

She now understood that if we build character, if we build self understanding, if we build emotional intelligence, we give kids the life tools and strategies to help them in many areas of their lives as well as school. These tools and strategies include how to:

- combat bullying at school and later in the workplace
- develop quality relationships
- interact with others successfully
- understand themselves, their partners and their families better
- take control of their lives
- succeed in the workplace
- create success in their life.

So Miss Young decided to embark upon a program to develop the hidden curriculum into her teaching. On a quiet Sunday afternoon she printed off a list of her year nine maths students and ranked them for 'Success Mindset'.

She prepared the following rubric and scored each student out of 5 for each attribute giving a possible total of 35 points. This is what she ended up with:

Student Name	Being Prepared	Being On Time	Self Motivated	Accepts Help	Work Ethic	Pride In Work	Self Reflective	Success Score
Tess	5	5	3	1	5	5	3	27
Bree	5	5	4	3	4	4	4	29
Sonya	2	1	1	2	1	1	1	9
Tom	1	1	1	2	1	1	1	8
Will	1	4	2	3	2	2	1	15
Meg	3	1	1	2	1	1	1	10
Kayla	1	4	1	1	1	2	2	12
Jake	5	5	2	4	4	3	3	30
Syd	5	4	4	3	4	4	1	25
Josh	3	3	3	5	3	3	2	22
Nikki	5	5	4	3	5	4	3	29
Anna	4	4	2	2	2	3	2	19
Rob	2	1	3	5	5	4	3	23
Beth	4	1	4	2	4	5	3	23
Danni	5	5	5	5	5	4	3	32
Julia	5	4	5	3	5	5	4	31
Alli	5	5	3	4	4	2	3	26
Dean	3	3	2	4	3	2	2	19
Abe	2	3	1	3	3	1	1	14
Felicity	4	4	3	4	4	3	3	25
Izzy	1	2	4	1	2	4	2	16
Jack	4	3	3	4	3	2	2	21
Ben	5	4	4	4	4	3	3	28
Tran	5	5	5	3	4	4	2	28

This exercise helped Miss Young identify where many of her students were failing in the hidden curriculum. She noticed that the kids who scored poorly in the hidden curriculum were the ones that struggled with the academic curriculum and therefore were not likely to develop the success mindset that would set them up for success after they finished school. She had experienced that with her own peers from secondary college. The slack kids who had been unpunctual, poorly motivated and refused to work, carried on those same attitudes post Year 12 and either couldn't be bothered to get a job or ended up bouncing from one job to the next.

Others were similar to what Miss Young had been like, dragging themselves to work every day and spending their lives whinging and complaining about how 'life sucks' at work. There were others who were rearing children on their own and had never been employed, friends in drug and alcohol rehabilitation centers and quite a number who had gained entry into university but had never completed their course.

At that moment Miss Young knew she had to try to make a meaningful difference in the lives of the students in her year nine maths class. She knew it wasn't going to be easy and that she wouldn't 'win them all' but she also knew that for those that bought into the program, it would be a life changing part of their education.

The success mindset program Miss Young constructed was adapted from what she had seen her brother do in the Scout Movement. It was similar to the Scout badge system as students were given **choices** as to which 'success' skills they worked on. When they successfully completed a skill development program they were awarded a Certificate of Excellence in that skill. Just being competent wasn't going to be good enough. The aim was for excellence. Miss Young didn't realize it at the time, but these certificates became valuable evidence of skill competency when her students started looking for part time jobs. Employers were impressed that students had trained in work related competencies and met high standards to achieve their certificates.

Success 4 Life Program

To introduce the Success 4 Life Program Miss Young decided to conduct a full class discussion on student mindset and she arranged for a visit from a student's (Nikki) father to help set the scene.

Nikki's dad, Graeme, worked at a nearby prison and knew only too well how easy it was for teenagers to get drawn into unhealthy habits and poor behaviours while at school and even after leaving school. By the time they ran into Graeme at the prison, it was all too late to do anything about it because they had already come to the attention of the police and been convicted.

Miss Young was hoping that by having Graeme talk to Nikki's classmates before they got themselves into trouble, they would choose to buy into her Success 4 Life Program to improve themselves. What Miss Young didn't realize was that Graeme had decided to bring along a nineteen year old prison inmate called Tim who had been a previous student at that very school. Tim told the class how he had lost focus and played up at school and thought everything would be alright when he left school and got a job. Tim explained how he had developed a drinking habit from his early teens and all his money went on booze. He started missing work, lost his job and ended up living on the streets in Melbourne. He scrounged meals from the Salvos and collected aluminum cans from rubbish bins just to stay alive and then one day he had a chance meeting with an old school mate.

The pair got on the booze together, decided to rob a Four Eleven store together and got caught in the act. Tim was serving five months jail for his part and explained how he felt his problems all started when he was in year nine. This was a powerful example to the class of just what can happen if kids allow negative habits into their lives. By this stage you could hear a pin drop in Miss Young's classroom as her students were confronted with a real life story of just how easy it is to fall into trouble. Statistics tell us that on average 33.2% of Miss Young's class were drinking alcohol (www.betterhealth.vic.gov.au) and Graeme went on to point out how irresponsible use of alcohol, especially as teenagers, can lead to impaired judgement and poor decision making with:

- binge drinking and the dangerous spin off of alcohol poisoning
- drink driving while unlicensed
- unsafe sex practices
- injury or death from risky behaviour or even suicide.

The visit from Graeme and Tim had a big impact on Miss Young's class. She followed up the discussion by explaining to her class how important it was for Year 9 students to develop successful work habits and that those habits would support them for the rest of their lives and help keep them out of trouble.

Miss Young then outlined how she was introducing a voluntary program called **Success 4 Life** to her year nine maths class. The program aimed at helping students develop personal and work habits that would support them at school and after they left school and entered the workforce. It would run parallel to the academic curriculum and included 15 units, each one designed to develop competency and excellence in skills to improve mindset and work skills. Students could choose if they wanted to be involved and which units they wished to study. When satisfactorily completed each unit would earn the student a Certificate of Excellence in that unit.

Let's have a brief look at what the students were offered.

Success 4 Life Program Units of Study

1. Certificate in Diary Management

This certificate required students to complete either a written diary **or** a digital diary for 10 weeks. The diary was to be graded on the following competencies:

- consistently neat diary entries
- daily entries including school assessment deadlines
- well organised notes and actions
- well kept contact list
- system of feedback notes and comments

Students were required to accumulate at least 45 points out of 50 possible to be assessed as competent.

2.   Certificate in Precise Punctuality

This certificate required students to be punctual for one full term of 10 weeks. A Record of Punctuality was to be completed on a daily basis on the following competencies:

- on time for class
- on time with homework
- on time with assessments
- on time for meetings
- on time for school

Students were required to accumulate at least 45 points out of 50 possible to be assessed as competent.

3.   Certificate in Outstanding Organisation

This certificate required students to be exceptionally well organised for 10 weeks. A Record of Organisation Sheet was to be completed on a daily basis on the following competencies:

- well prepared for class with texts, stationary, tools and equipment
- correct uniform for appropriate class
- well prepared for special classes such as Phys Ed and Home Eco
- evidence of thorough preparation for tests and exams
- consistently keeps effective class notes
- consistently brings items from home as required
- high standard of locker organisation

Students were required to accumulate at least 45 points out of 50 possible to be assessed as competent.

4. Certificate in Personal Conduct

This certificate required students to conduct themselves at an excellent standard for 10 weeks. A Record of Personal Conduct was to be completed on a daily basis in the following competencies:

- courteous manner to others
- excellent manners when speaking
- behaves appropriate to the situation
- considerate of others in the classroom
- considerate of teachers (five teachers to sign off)

Students were required to accumulate at least 45 points out of 50 possible to be assessed as competent.

5. Certificate in Work Habits

This certificate required students to sustain a high level of productive work habits for 10 weeks. A Record of Work Habits was to be completed on a daily basis on the following competencies:

- evidence of excellence at independent work
- consistently dedicated at improving their learning
- excellent team worker
- excellent standard of class notes
- highly productive use of class time

Students were required to accumulate at least 45 points out of 50 possible to be assessed as competent.

6. Certificate in Persistent Attitude

This certificate required students to show excellence in persistence for 10 weeks. A Record of Persistence was to be completed on a daily basis on the following competencies:

- exhibits a 'have a go' attitude at all times
- consistently uses mistakes as learning opportunities
- regularly acts on feedback
- looks for alternative ways to solve problems
- shows determination to succeed

Students were required to accumulate at least 45 points out of 50 possible to be assessed as competent.

7. Certificate in Public Speaking

This certificate required students to show a high level of public speaking at least twice in each of the following competencies:

- speaking in front of class
- making a presentation on a school issue to a staff meeting
- making a video presentation on a community issue
- making an oral presentation in a community forum
- making a presentation at a whole school assembly

Students were required to accumulate at least 45 points out of 50 possible to be assessed as competent.

8. Certificate In Goal Setting

This certificate required students to write, implement and complete two goals using the SMART goal setting system:

- choosing goals that are Specific, Measurable, Achievable, Realistic and to a Timeframe
- writing goals using the SMART format
- implementing goals and successfully negotiating obstacles and sourcing the resources needed
- completing goals on time and assessing the success or failure of the goal
- rewarding oneself for achieving goals

Students were required to accumulate at least 45 points out of 50 possible to be assessed as competent in Goal Setting.

9. Certificate in Mentoring

This certificate required students to prove competence in mentoring others in the following five areas:
- another student with homework
- a younger student with wellbeing
- a pre school child in 'baby sitting'
- a teacher by providing feedback on teacher strategies
- an adult family member on how they can support kids at school

Students were required to accumulate at least 45 points out of 50 possible to be assessed as competent.

10. Certificate in Voluntary Work

This certificate required students to prove competence at voluntary work in each of the following areas:

- volunteering help in the classroom
- volunteering help for the school
- volunteering help for a local community club or charity
- a research project into a national charity
- operate a fund raising activity for an accepted charity

Students were required to accumulate at least 45 points out of 50 possible to be assessed as competent.

11. Certificate in Leadership

This certificate required students to prove strong leadership skills in the following areas:

- self leadership
- leadership of one other- mentoring
- team or group leadership in class
- leadership on a school excursion or camp
- leadership in a community based organisation

Students were required to accumulate at least 45 points out of 50 possible to be assessed as competent.

12. Certificate in Personal Care

This certificate required students to show outstanding levels of personal care for 10 weeks. A Checklist of Personal Care attributes was to be completed on a daily basis on the following competencies:

- clean hands and face for full school day
- clean nails kept within school nail standards
- well kept shoes
- uniform and clothes well cared for
- hair well groomed and within school hair policy

Students were required to accumulate at least 45 points out of 50 possible to be assessed as competent.

Full details of the Success 4 Life Program can be obtained from www. DynamicTeachingTools.com

The uptake for the Success 4 Life Program was patchy at first, but it wasn't long before the first certificates were being awarded and then a Bronze Badge. Miss Young had included another adaption from the Scout program her brother had completed. But instead of having Second Class, First Class and Queen Scouts, Miss Young used Bronze, Silver and Gold Badges. When students completed any four certificates of choice they received their Bronze Badge. If they completed eight certificates of choice they received their Silver Badge. If they chose to complete all 12 certificates, they received their Gold Badge and the Diploma of Mindset Success which qualified them to become a Success 4 Life Assessor.

Apart from the initial setup, Miss Young found the program surprisingly easy to implement with those in the class that chose to get involved. She had been concerned at the extra workload with keeping track of the assessments but most the units seemed to fit seamlessly into normal classroom life and the interest and excitement the program gave the students made the assessments a joy. Students used their certificates on their resumes and suddenly stories started coming back to class of employers who gave credibility to the kids' certificates. More and more kids entered the program. Other kids from other classes heard about the program and wanted to get in on the action and so the program snowballed across the whole year nine cohort.

There was a story Miss Young told the class of a year 12 student from the previous year who missed a final VCE English exam because he thought it was on Thursday when actually it was on Wednesday. That exam was worth 50% of his final grading. His whole year's work was seriously affected because he hadn't been taught tools like keeping a diary and being punctual. Students started seeing the certificates as being worthwhile and helpful in their lives.

Suddenly kids like Beth, Will and Kayla were setting goals to improve their punctuality and submitting work on time. They mentored each other and each set up a diary to record the times they got to class. At the end of each week they would review their diary and calculate the percentage of classes they made it to on time and graph the results. Their punctuality graphs started climbing steeply and keeping a diary became an important tool to help them.

All students commencing their chosen unit were asked to write a goal. You will notice below how this goal setting process introduces the goal as having already been achieved. Students Sonya, Meg and Abe set the following Work Ethic goal:

Friday 13th March

It is now three thirty on Friday the Twenty Sixth of June 2015 and Sonya, Meg and Abe are excited to have successfully completed the Certificate of Work Effort. We feel happy and satisfied that we have learnt a lot about successful work habits.

Steps we need to take to achieve our goal:

1. Prove we can each work independently in maths
2. Concentrate on improving at maths
3. Work as a team to complete our goal
4. Keep neat and extensive class notes in maths
5. Work hard in class
6. Use feedback to help us improve

Obstacles

- Can't understand the maths
- Other kids distracting us

Back up plan

Ask for help, after school maths help

Work together and support each other

Who and what do I need to assist me:

1. Miss Young to keep us accountable for our goal and explain the maths to us
2. Each other to work as a team
3. Completion of The Record Of Work Habits

How strong is our intention to take the first step?   1 2 3 4 5 6 7 8 9 ⑩

How strong is our enthusiasm to take the first step?   1 2 3 4 5 6 7 8 9 ⑩

How strong is my commitment to take the first step?   1 2 3 4 5 6 7 8 9 ⑩

The Success 4 Life Program became a huge success for Miss Young's year nine maths class.

Its main benefits were:

- it was easy for the kids to use
- the students could see a purpose in it
- it gave kids choice so they could match it to their needs and interests
- students could see themselves improving
- employers loved the training modules and complimented the kids on them
- it empowered the kids to take ownership of what they felt they needed to improve at.

Miss Young has now become a true educator rather than just a teacher. She is now facilitating student learning rather than forcing learning through authoritarian means. Students now felt empowered about their time in maths class and this change of mindset supported their academic endeavors as well. But more importantly, self improvement became a dominant theme in Miss Young's classes and the skills and strategies the students were learning in the hidden curriculum developed character, pride in work, a sense of achievement and a positive work ethic.

Chapter 5 Resources:

1. The 'Success 4 Life' Program. Available for Teacher Members and School Members at www.DynamicTeachingTools.com

2. www.betterhealth.vic.gov.au

3. Go to the www.DynamicTeachingTools.com website to download a free Goal Setting template for students.

What's This About Self Science?

"As family life no longer offers growing numbers of children a sure footing in life, schools are left as the one place communities can turn to for correctives to children's deficiencies in social and emotional competence."

(Daniel Goleman in his book 'Emotional Intelligence')

Chapter Six

What's This About Self Science?

For the students in Miss Young's maths class the school's expectation is for her to deliver the approved curriculum to the best of her ability. We saw in the previous chapter how important the hidden curriculum can be in supporting student academic success. But there is yet another side to teaching in the 21st century which is also much more than an exchange of academic curriculum between teacher and student. In fact these days, there is a breakdown of traditional family structures and constant exposure of students to electronic media, social media, videos and computer games. This causes a deficit of moral support and guidance for so many kids, therefore the teacher's role has become much more one of providing wellbeing and emotional support for students.

We have seen close up the problems and issues students bring to Miss Young's class. If she doesn't help these students with basic wellbeing issues, then who does? While most schools these days do have some sort of wellbeing system to support students when they meet problems, it is still the teachers who bear the brunt of the wellbeing issues which impact so emphatically on student learning in the classroom.

This brings me to the sad story of a successful student I shall call Charlie. Despite attending a very average rural secondary school, and despite what appeared to be quite an indifferent attitude towards VCE (Victorian Certificate of Education), Charlie scored an ATAR (Australian Tertiary Admission Rank) score of 97.8 (out of 99.99) and was dux of his year. He was clearly a gifted academic student but there was something missing. Charlie's ATAR score never quite got him directly into the medicine course he applied for, but he did commence a university course which gave him the opportunity to step up into medicine if his marks in first year warranted it.

However, Charlie was completely unprepared for independent life from an emotional intelligence perspective. Unfortunately, the drug salesman down the end of the street was a better salesman than Charlie's teachers and parents, and by saying this I mean no disrespect to Charlie's parents or his teachers. During his VCE years, Charlie dabbled with drugs which led him into minor dealing and associating with people who were not acting in Charlie's best interests.

When Charlie went off to Melbourne to begin his tertiary studies, hopes were high. He soon landed a part time job at a bar but unfortunately for Charlie, that led him further into temptation. Together with the excitement and freedom that moving out of home and university life offered him, Charlie's life quickly spiraled out of control. He continued using and dealing; he began drinking heavily and he wasn't paying attention to his studies. By mid year Charlie had dropped out of university and was admitted to a drug rehabilitation centre.

Ten years later Charlie is but a shadow of the former brilliant student. Years of drug induced violent outbursts mixed up with broken relationships and periods of enforced imprisonment in drug rehabilitation facilities, has destroyed him physically, mentally and emotionally.

He lives alone, brain damaged and bitter and spends a good day at home watching the traffic go by, and a bad day locked up to dry out again. He is only 30 years old and our education system missed an opportunity to equip Charlie with the self science skills to support him to fulfill his potential. Self science is the study of emotional intelligence which in turn supports and empowers the holistic wellbeing of students.

Which brings us to the question, is it a teacher's role to teach self science at school? Some say it is not. There are teachers out there who feel this is an area where expert guidance from psychologists and youth counselors is the better way to go and I agree that psychologists and counselors will be part of this solution. But teachers are in the right spot to make a huge difference.

Teachers know the kids well, they have built relationships with them and they are in the perfect position to use everyday incidents and issues as valuable self science learning experiences for students. Many teachers already do this to some extent and they should. All the academic progress in the world is useless if kids unravel socially and emotionally and there is a lot of research suggesting that this is a growing problem. As an example, research from Beyond Blue shows us, "In 2013, almost one in four young people (24.3%) said they were sad, very sad or not happy when asked to report how happy they were with their life as a whole." (https://www.youthbeyondblue.com/footer/stats-and-facts)

Chloe Madanes, a world leader in helping kids with emotional intelligence says, "You don't need a PhD to change a life. You just need the right strategies." So let's equip our teachers like Miss Young with some simple strategies that can easily be incorporated into everyday life in the classroom and encourage them to take the time to make a difference through the art of self science.

The Art of Self Science

Self science is all about equipping students with the social and emotional skills to thrive at school and later in modern society. It is about prevention and it helps kids to develop tools and strategies that give them choices when dealing with issues in their life. For example, if a child understands how to deal with conflict other than through being too passive or over aggressive, then he is better placed to coach himself through a conflict incident without resorting to violence or submission. The following points explain some strategies that will help promote the art of self science.

1. How To Develop Simple Student Emotional Intelligence Strategies

    •   Help students to identify and label feelings in a whole range of different areas such as body language, facial expressions, spoken language, written language, art and music. The understanding of how to identify and label their own feelings, as well as the feelings

of others, supports children to be more tolerant and understanding of other people. This can only help them to protect themselves and be compassionate towards others.

- Educate students on how to express their feelings in a variety of ways that will empower them rather than cause them harm, such as verbally, physically, facially, in writing, in art, in music. This skill helps students communicate their feelings in a therapeutic way which supports their emotional wellbeing.
- Teach kids how to measure the intensity of feelings within themselves and in others and thereby be able to gauge which reactions are appropriate to which situations.
- Learning the concept of delayed gratification is an important skill for teenagers to develop. In a period in their life when impulsive behaviour mixed with a need to prove independence prevails, it will help if teenagers can learn that experimenting with smoking, drugs and alcohol might give them a short term high at the cost of long term addictions and associated health problems.
- Helping kids to control the impulses to act without thinking, to fight, to buy, to laugh, to cry, to complain is useful. Simple impulse control games such as 'Simon Says', memory games such as 'Who Am I?' and role plays will help develop understanding and application of impulse control skills.
- Teaching students how to reduce stress through strategies such as controlled breathing, laughter therapy, getting active, thought control and visualization are simple but powerful strategies that will assist them.

2. Simple Ways To Build Effective Cognitive Strategies

- Help students use the inner voice as a positive force. That 'little voice' inside our heads can be a destructive force if negative stories and scripts are allowed to develop. Teaching kids how to turn the 'I can't...' thoughts into 'I can...' thoughts just by adding the word yet to 'I can't' is a very simple and effective tool to build cognitive strategies. "I can't do algebra" is a destructive story, but "I can't do algebra yet" is full of hope and determination.

- Understanding and interpreting social cues is another critical cognitive skill for children to learn. Cues such as making eye contact, reading body language and noticing changes in voice tone and volume help kids to read social situations and understand how to behave in different situations.

- Teaching kids structured problem solving and decision making strategies using tools such as the De Bono thinking hats, goal setting, identifying alternative actions, anticipating consequences and sourcing help will also help to strengthen the emotional intelligence muscle.

- Helping kids understand another's perspectives will be of great benefit. A key strategy to aid development of this skill is to ask students to critique other students doing a role play. It not only helps kids to understand another's perspective, but it exposes them to a range of strategies they may not have experienced.

- Teaching understanding of behavioural norms and what is acceptable and what is not in different situations is important. Kids need to learn to accept that there is a time and a place for different behaviours. Using ipads appropriately in the classroom is a valuable tool to teach this cognitive skill. If we ban the ipads, we lose the opportunity to teach appropriate behaviour.

- Helping kids develop self awareness and realistic expectations about themselves is vital. Developing a child's self awareness is all about helping them understand and recognize their strengths and weaknesses. Once they are aware of them they can create realistic expectations for themselves.

3. Strategies To Develop Social Behavioural Skills

- The use of body language to communicate with others is an important tool for children to learn. Teachers and parents are the role models from whom our kids learn this behaviour. But simple teaching

activities showing kids how to maintain personal space, how to use eye contact, how to use a smile and facial expressions, how to shake hands, how to use hand gestures for communicating are valuable life tools for them.

- Verbal behaviour is yet another plank of social behavioural skills. Teaching our children tools such as how to ask effective questions, make clear requests, respond effectively to criticism, manipulate voice tone and volume will be worthwhile activities for teaching social behavioural intelligence.

- Teaching kids how to resist negative social influences, listen actively to others, be proactive at helping others and participate in positive peer groups will all be useful tools for kids to learn. If a teacher can create a really positive and proactive group in a class, this can be so effective at generating goodwill from the other students that a lot of the inter-student tension will melt away.

- Teaching conflict resolution skills will also be valuable strategies for students to learn and this includes learning to understand and deal with inner conflict as well as learning how to avoid and resolve conflict with others. In his book, 'How To Win Friends And Influence People' Dale Carnegie gives us a simple lesson to teach kids how to resolve an argument. "The only way to get the best of an argument is to avoid it." Simply agree with your opponent and there will be no argument! Try it, it works and it will work for kids too.

The benefits of spending school time on these subjects have been proven time and time again by research into schools and education systems that have invested time and energy into them. They can be infiltrated through normal academic programs and taught with simple lessons as the need arises.

The second part of teaching Self Science in schools is to develop strategies for kids to use to improve their own wellbeing.

Essential Lessons in Student Wellbeing

Student wellbeing is defined by the University of Melbourne as "a state of positive psychological functioning that allows students to thrive, flourish and learn. Wellbeing refers to a state of positive emotional and social functioning that we would wish to nurture in all our students." (www.web.education. unimelb.edu.au/swap/wellbeing)

I don't agree with this definition. To me student wellbeing has a much more holistic, all encompassing definition. It is much more about educating students to look after their whole being, not just their psychological functioning.

So to me a holistic wellbeing program for schools would include all students working on the following skills on a daily basis:

1. Learning how to take responsibility for their health through:

    *   giving healthy eating choices at the school canteen
    *   offering breakfast options to all students
    *   encouraging healthy drinking habits- I'm not talking about alcohol consumption I'm talking about drinking water and avoiding high sugar drinks
    *   training in treating cuts, bruises and burns as they occur
    *   training in toileting hygiene, dental hygiene and hygiene of ears, eyes, nose, mouth and hands
    *   keeping bodies clean and nails and hair well attended
    *   caring for themselves when they are sick and knowing what to do
    *   monitoring health and growth.

2. Learning how to create a daily physical fitness and coordination program that includes:

    *   a daily exercise program for 20 minutes. Give students a choice of the exercise programs available to them. For example, a skipping program, calisthenics, walking, running, gymnastics etc

- a 5 minute physical coordination exercise program rotating around rope skipping, balance exercises, hand eye coordination activities with a ball, throwing at a target, calisthenics
- breathing exercises involving breath control, deep breathing, breathing cycles and breathing to our walking speed
- monitoring fitness progress by assessing and recording improvements in skills, repetitions, exercise activities, strength and blood pressure.

3. Learning how to look after and train the brain on a daily basis through:

- developing 'brain food' eating programs designed to meet the specific needs of the individual student. Learning which foods to avoid and which foods to include to match personal needs can be life changing for students
- mental gymnastics exercises such as playing, 'Who Am I?', or 'Simon Says' or, "Charades' are great for exercising the brain muscle
- memory exercises such as repeating number sequences forwards and backwards. For example, ask the child to repeat these numbers in order and then repeat them backwards. (362789, 987263)
- practicing different learning techniques such as learning by listening, learning by watching, learning by doing or even learning with a partner
- brain training physical exercises such as reverse windmills and hand locks will also assist students to exercise both sides of their brain
- logic and thinking puzzles such as Suduko, crosswords, word searches all stimulate brain activity and train the brain.

4. Learning how to promote improved family relationships through effective communication strategies with:

- parents
- siblings
- grandparents
- babies
- step family
- aunts, uncles, cousins and far flung family.

5. Learning the basics for social interaction with others such as:

    *   meeting people for the first time
    *   social safety when shopping
    *   staying safe on our roads
    *   safety at parties
    *   cyber safety
    *   matching social behaviour to different situations. For example, funerals, car accidents, sport, church.

6. Learning how to contribute to others to improve personal wellbeing through:

    *   offering to help
    *   volunteering to organise or lead
    *   giving to the needy
    *   supporting charities

7. Learning about Financial Management:

Money is such an integral part of living in the 21st century and such a trigger for disharmony in relationships and family. Financial literacy is vital for every students' wellbeing training. The Moneysmart Teaching Program introduced by the Australian Securities and Investment Commission is an excellent program for developing financial literacy skills at school. It develops a foundation of basic skills in primary school and builds on them year after year well into secondary school with strategies such as:

*   learning basic money counting skills
*   learning how to develop effective saving habits
*   learning to understand spending habits
*   different ways of earning an income
*   how superannuation works
*   how taxation works
*   making informed financial decisions in the home

- buying a home
- how loans work
- investment strategies.

8.   Learning about road sense:

Road sense and driver etiquette can be a regular learning experience right from when our kids are young. Pedestrian etiquette starts when kids are just toddlers and is certainly not helped when parents walk against the 'Don't Walk' sign with their kids in tow. Toddler's brains simply cannot make safe judgements about crossing the road so they copy what their parents do. Walking against the lights becomes a very quick negative lesson to children that road signs don't really apply to them. School lessons teaching road sense are life long lessons that will support students as they become active road users with:

- riding bikes
- riding scooters
- pedestrians rights and responsibilities
- driving rules and responsibilities .

One of the great benefits to society of improving student wellbeing and emotional intelligence will come when they become parents of the next generation of kids. Their kids will learn self science from them. Then we will start to see the generational change that is needed to arrest some of the negative social issues that are affecting society today.

Essential Lessons For Teachers (and Parents) About Student Wellbeing

Todd's work with Miss Young helped her develop a deeper understanding of how kids operate and how to utilise that understanding with the students she worked with. She learnt that kids do not have adult brains and so it was not sensible for her to expect them to behave with the self control and maturity of a 30 year old. It also helped her to understand that kids' brains go through growth cycles which last roughly three years. She now understood that their learning will often happen in spits and spurts rather than a smooth upward curve and would roughly follow a timeframe, such as:

- From birth to about three years old, kids brains are highly active and 'sponges' for learning and copying adult behavior.
- The brains of four to six year olds seem to want to ask 'why' every second word and will benefit from learning about impulse control.
- At age seven to nine, kids brains go through a learning surge in language development.
- At about 10 to 12 years of age kids become more peer oriented and bullying and bitchiness become part of their challenges in life.
- At about age 12 kids' brains start to slow down as they commence a period of major reconstruction and by the time they hit Miss Young's Year 9 maths class their brains and bodies are undergoing fundamental reconstruction and change. Understanding this helped Miss Young to keep the behaviour of her class in perspective rather than take it as a personal affront.
- By 14 to 16 years of age the frontal lobe of adolescent brains are 'closed for construction', leaving previously sane, common sense kids behaving completely differently through poor impulse control, planning difficulties and being inconsiderate of others' feelings. As well, hormones are running rife through these teenage bodies causing emotional and irritable students.

"This means that teenagers' brains are all tuned up for emotions, fighting, running away and romance but not so well tuned up for planning, controlling impulses and forward thinking."

(Andrew Fuller)

And what does Miss Young expect of the Year 9 students in her classroom? Good planning, good self-control and forward thinking! This is a challenge the Miss Youngs of this world face, because, like it or not, teachers are in fact fulfilling the role of these kids' frontal lobes and so are their parents.

- By 18 to 20 years old, kids' brains have turned the corner and their behaviour has almost become human again. The challenges for these kids are to establish a positive identity and understanding of where they are in their life, and to establish a good supportive group of friends.
- The brains of 21 to 24 year olds are almost completely reconfigured with the finishing touches being put on their sense of independence and their goals for their future.

So Miss Young took onboard this understanding and set to work at improving the wellbeing of the students in her classes. She studied the work of child psychologist Andrew Fuller and learnt that the biggest barrier for most students to doing well at school is not their attitude, intelligence or motivation it is their levels of anxiety.

This view of Andrew's was backed up from research by Resilient Youth Australia (www.resilientyouth.org.au) which found that 25% of girls and 21% of boys feel anxious and under strain and that these levels rise to 69% of girls and 36% of boys by Year 12.

Miss Young also learnt that problems with elevated stress levels were accompanied by sleep and concentration problems, memory difficulties and distractibility, not to mention a lessening of the joy of learning, all issues that would impact on student learning in her classroom.

As Andrew Fuller put it, "Great schools nurture great souls. Education is about much more than just the marks. You can be good at passing the test but be bad at life. If we allow the international rat race of PISA results and national testing programs to narrow our focus we will have collateral damage. The cost will come in a lessening of imagination, courage, character and empowerment. The result on one specific test is transitory. The attitude people take towards learning has life long consequences."

Miss Young learnt from Andrew Fuller, the following strategies for improving student wellbeing:

- Mistakes are opportunities for growth, not for shaming students. Shame causes low motivation. Some kids feel it is better to opt out rather than to endure humiliation.
Classrooms should be more about questions and less about answers. Many people say they learn more from their failures than their successes. Try using guestimation games, quizzes, puzzles, mazes, mysteries, forensic clues and problem solving games to build a have-a-go mindset. Ask students to tell you a wrong answer and to give you one reason they think it might be wrong.
- Mindfulness is about being aware and being present. Now! Creating rituals where everyone can stop and bring their energies and their awareness into the present will improve outcomes and lessen anxiety. We can achieve this by focusing less on the results and more on awareness and commitment.
- Use relaxation and focusing methods including guided relaxation, brain gym, breathing exercises, creative problem solving, yoga, drama games, visualisation, colouring, sport, chanting and body mathematics to empower kids to develop wellbeing tools.
- Exercise, sports, and rhythmic activities help students to energise and focus their brains. Use the increased presence of mind and focus to empower students to develop skills through resilience based coaching. In resilience based coaching, everyone in a school (staff, parents, students) is asked to take on an area to improve upon each term. One of the mottos we use is, "Here everyone gets smart".
The process is to have each person select an area to focus on and rate their current level on a ten point scale (10 = totally awesome to 1= dreadfully incompetent). They are then asked to describe what it would look like if they were two points further up that scale. What would be happening differently?
They are then asked to focus on noticing when that happens. That's it. They aren't asked to work at it, develop improvement plans or have

additional coaching to make gains in that area. Just notice it when it occurs. Instead of focusing on the outcomes and results, direct your attention to what you need to do each day in order to get the results. Our energy follows our attention. If you can, review progress each term and then either select a new area to focus on or continue working on the current skill. Resilience based coaching reinforces the idea that schools are learning communities where everyone can get better at things.

- Open learning areas work well in some settings but can be factories for anxiety in others. Sixteen percent of students will have hearing problems to the extent that they will be unable to hear in an open learning area. Creative, independent thinking is often harder in noisy, distracting circumstances. Students who have traumatic backgrounds, have been bullied at schools, have family difficulties or are new arrivals to the country often report higher levels of anxiety in open learning settings. When you are anxious, your levels of cortisol and adrenaline increase, blood is shifted away from your brain and you are focused on survival rather than learning.

- There are some wonderful apps that can be used to help schools implement relaxation and focusing programs. Two of Andrew's favourites are Brainwaves and Buddify.

- When students and their parents learn about how their brain works they have a choice. Learning about what drives anxiety and how to shift your gears down is useful information. Also, learning that you can't believe all of your thoughts and that some of your feelings are pretty shifty too, helps people to start thinking about their 'thinking' rather than just being a victim of the latest idea that flies into their heads. Anxiety is a sign of an overloaded brain. It is toxic to creativity and memory. Learning the signs of stress and knowing what to do to come back to a state of relaxed focus is a skill everyone needs. We all need good refreshing sleep to learn well. It is a revelation to some people that if you start your day either by denying yourself some fuel or by having a few energy drinks and a bowl of chips you might feel like something has crawled into your head and died there by midmorning!

- Let's make happiness the key goal of schools. Happiness is the antidote to anxiety. Little kids move, play, explore and question. Then they are told to sit down and do some hard work called learning. When we put the playfulness back into learning, motivation and engagement increase and performance improves dramatically.

  When students are encouraged to take risks, play, create and learn, neuroplasticity increases. If we combine this with good sleep, nutrition and enough physical movement, learning outcomes soar.

(The above lessons for teachers and parents about student wellbeing are courtesy of Andrew Fuller: www.andrewfuller.com)

In his book, 'Emotional Intelligence', Daniel Goleman summarises layer after layer of research which has identified the benefits of teaching Self Science in schools:

- improved **emotional self awareness** in things like recognizing and naming emotions, understanding the causes of feelings and recognizing the difference between feelings and actions
- better at **managing emotions** such as frustration, anger and sadness leading to less aggressive or self-destructive behaviour, improved handling of stress and social anxiety
- fewer school suspensions and expulsions and **improved attitudes** towards school
- increased skill at **harnessing emotions,** productively by taking responsibility, showing self control and focusing on the task at hand
- **greater empathy** at considering other's perspectives, feelings and decisions
- **improved relationships** through better conflict resolution, negotiation skills and understanding of how relationships work
- more popular with peers, **more cooperative**, more democratic, more considerate, more outgoing

As a result, kids became:

- more responsible
- more assertive
- more popular and outgoing
- more pro-social and outgoing
- better at understanding others
- more considerate
- better at social strategies for interpersonal problem solving
- more harmonious
- more 'democratic'
- better at conflict resolution.

As a consequence, significant improvements in student academic standards were recorded in the participating schools:

- up to 50% of students showed improved achievement scores
- up to 38% of students improved their grade averages
- incidents of misbehaviour dropped an average of 28% including suspensions down by 44%
- attendance rates rose and 63% of students demonstrated more positive behaviour towards school

How can we ignore these results?

A benefit of our work in Self Science will be to help kids learn how to find answers to the following questions:

1. Who am I? What do I like most about me? What is my sense of purpose? Where am I going? How will I get there? Who is going with me? What do I need to learn? How will I measure success?
2. What are my gifts? If I could leave a 'mark' what would it look like? What rewards am I really seeking? What training do I need to be at my best? How much is enough? What is my legacy?

3. What matters to me most? How do I love myself and remain my own best friend? What are the bonds I honour most in my life? How do I attach to others? Am I a good friend to others? How is my love evolving and growing? What would add value to my expressions of intimacy?

4. How does my mind wander outside the box? How do I have fun being me? What are my favorite forms of spontaneous expression? How am I creative? What learning would deepen my creativity? With which friends am I the most creative and playful?

5. What am I doing here? What can I rely on? How do I arrive at inner peace? What are my basic beliefs and how do I express them? What do I feel called to do with my life? How do I express reverence for life?

6. What is my legacy? What will live on after I'm gone? How can I support the needs of others? What are the most important contributions I make? What causes am I willing to support? How can I volunteer my time to make a difference?

Self Science is powerful stuff that needs our attention.

Chapter 6 Resources:

1. Beyond Blue (www.youthbeyondblue.com/footer/stats-and-facts)

2. The Art of Self Science Teacher Development Program (www.DynamicTeacherTools.com)

3. Recommended Reading:
   - 'How To Win Friends And Influence People', Dale Carnegie
   - 'Emotional Intelligence', Daniel Goleman
   - 'Tricky Kids', Andrew Fuller

4. Moneysmart Teaching (www.asic.com.au)

5. Andrew Fuller (www.andrewfuller.com)

The Alphabet Kids

> "Children by nature are caring; nastiness and exclusion are learned traits."
>
> **(Randa Habelrih in 'Dealing With Autism')**

Chapter Seven

The Alphabet Kids

Miss Young's Year 9 maths class contained three 'alphabet kids' who had been diagnosed with a disability and therefore qualified for extra funding. There was Tom diagnosed with ADHD (Attention Deficit Hyperactive Disorder), Dean with NVLD (Non Verbal Learning Disorder) and Jack suffering from ASD (Autism Spectrum Disorder). The school used the funding attached to these students to employ a team of Student Support Officers (SSOs are sometimes called LSO's or Learning Support Officers) to assist teachers to run modified programs for these kids. But that didn't mean that Miss Young had three SSOs helping in her maths class, simply because the funding didn't stretch that far. There were times when Miss Young might have one SSO helping out but there also times when she had none.

The old Miss Young had told herself the story that she wasn't trained to teach special needs kids and in a classroom setting it was impossible for her to cater for these kids when there were 21 other students with all their myriad of abilities and issues to deal with. There were times when Tom, Dean and especially Jack, would have felt neglected. There were also times when Miss Young excluded Jack from class altogether because of his peculiar behaviour patterns and Tom for disruptive behaviour.

What Miss Young did do for alphabet students like Dean, Tom and Jack, was provide a modified program of special worksheets that were related to the topic the class was studying but at a simpler level. When an SSO was available they mainly helped this trio to complete their worksheets.

Having special needs kids with conditions such as autism, cerebral palsy, Opposition Defiant Disorder (ODD), dyslexia, ADHD, and the like in the classroom is only something that has crept into mainstream schools over the last 30 years or so. Back in the 1970's and '80's, most special needs kids were sent to special schools like Pleasant Creek Special School in Stawell. I worked

at Pleasant Creek for over 10 years teaching students with all sorts of physical, mental, social and emotional disabilities. This school serviced students from Pleasant Creek Training Centre and students with disabilities from the surrounding towns. The Training Centre was a live-in centre for students with disabilities from all over the state. This meant that back in those days, mainstream teachers were rarely seeing kids with these types of disabilities in their classrooms.

Things changed dramatically during the early '90's when Training Centres like Pleasant Creek and schools like Pleasant Creek Special School were closed and many of the clients were sent back to their parents to attend mainstream schools. This change in policy was backed up by legislation and has significantly increased the classroom expectation of teachers who often have no training at understanding the disabilities or how to teach students who have them.

The Disability Discrimination Act of 1992 makes this quite clear: "Educators must offer a person with a disability the same educational opportunities as everyone else. This means that if a person with a disability meets the necessary entry requirements of a school or college he or she should have just as much chance to study there as anyone else. Educators must base their decisions on a person's ability to meet the essential requirements of the course. They should not make assumptions about what a person can or cannot do because of a disability."

The Disability Discrimination Act was framed to protect students with a disability against discrimination in education in the following areas:

- Refusal or failure to accept an application for admission from a person with a disability.
- Accepting a person with a disability as a student on less favourable terms or conditions than others. For example, asking a person with a disability to pay higher fees.
- Denying or limiting access to people with a disability. For example, not allowing a person to attend excursions or join in school sports,

delivering lectures in an inaccessible format, inaccessible student common rooms.

- Expelling a person because of a disability, or subjecting a person with a disability to any other detriment.
- Humiliating comments or actions about a person's disability, such as insults, or comments or actions which create a hostile environment.

The Act also went on:

"If a person with a disability meets the essential entry requirements, then educators are required to make changes or reasonable adjustments if that person needs them to perform essential course-work.

Adjustments could include:

- Modifying educational premises. For example, making ramps, modifying toilets and ensuring that classes are in rooms accessible to the person with a disability.
- Modifying or providing equipment. For example, lowering lab benches, enlarging computer screens, providing specific computer software or an audio loop system.
- Changing assessment procedures. For example, allowing for alternative examination methods such as oral exams, or allowing additional time for someone else to write an exam for a person with a disability.
- Changing course delivery. For example, providing study notes or research materials in different formats or providing a sign language interpreter for a deaf person."

(Discussion Paper: 2015 Review of Disability Standards for Education)

In 2005, the Department of Education and Training further cemented the rights of disabled students in mainstream education when it released its 'Disability Standards for Education' policy which outlined the responsibilities of education providers towards kids with disabilities.

It is now 2015 and a review of these standards is being conducted. The introduction to that review confirms just how difficult it has become for teachers to effectively cater for special needs kids.

I quote, "The Australian Bureau of Statistics (ABS) notes that there are approximately 295,000 children in Australia of school age, between five and 17 years of age, who live with some form of disability. The majority of these students go to mainstream schools." (ABS, 2014).

The ABS' Survey of Disability, Ageing and Carers found that children living with disability, experience a number of difficulties with education. These include learning, social, and communication difficulties. Yet the ABS survey in 2012 reported that many children with profound disabilities receive less support in mainstream schools than they would in special schools. This remains the case for those young people continuing into the higher education and vocational sectors.

Almost one-third of submissions to the development of the National Disability Standards highlighted that "far from ensuring young people with disabilities have every opportunity to realise their potential, the education system acts as a barrier to greater achievement and independence in their lives." (Discussion Paper: 2015 Review of Disability Standards for Education)

The reality is that Miss Young and mainstream teachers in the 21st century are required to teach students suffering from a large spectrum of disabilities and learning difficulties which present special challenges. Many teachers have no training at all for working with students with autism, ADHD, sight, hearing and speech problems, cerebral palsy, language disorders, dyslexia and so on.

This puts teachers in a very difficult position. They have the needs of a whole classroom of students to consider and yet they find that one or two students can require a large portion of their time and attention.

For many classes it can be much more complex than that. If we look at Miss Young's Year 9 maths class there is Tom with ADHD, Dean with a Severe

Language Disorder, and Rob with Autism, plus Anna who is dealing with Anorexia, Danni who is struggling with her parents' separation and Beth who broke her arm playing netball. So Miss Young has a lot on her plate and that's only in her Year 9 maths class.

Then there is the reality that Miss Young's students have learning strengths and weaknesses. We all do. Some of us have more profound disabilities than others, but all students, and adults too, have weak areas. Having strengths and weaknesses is just part of being human and helping students understand and accept their weaknesses is an important role for a teacher. On the other hand, we all have strengths and special abilities so helping students, and this includes students with disabilities, find what they are uniquely abled at is also an important part of a teacher's job.

This is where the ground breaking work of Barbara Arrowsmith Young would make a huge difference to student learning across our country. The Arrowsmith Program is specifically designed to identify cognitive weaknesses in students and to strengthen them where appropriate with a program of exercises and activities.

Let's listen to Barbara Arrowsmith Young speak for a moment:

"We know that the brain is pliable and elastic, not fixed as we used to believe. It can physically change in response to stimulus and develop new neuronal branches and synaptic connections. This means that the brains of children with certain learning disabilities can be strengthened to the point of average or even above average functionality."

The program is truly remarkable. It's giving some traditionally disadvantaged children much brighter futures. They are able to reach their potential and progress alongside their peers in the regular stream.

How good would it be if this proactive method of improving learning outcomes for all students was adopted in a program where all early primary school

children were tested across the whole spectrum of cognitive abilities? Areas of weakness would be identified and then strengthened through a rigorous program that would help set up all students for academic success and thereby alleviate the frustration, embarrassment and harassment many students suffer because of preventable learning disabilities.

But let's get back to Miss Young's Year 9 maths class. The new, above the magic line Miss Young, knew she had to change her outlook towards the special needs students in her class. As a first step she made the time to read the notes that came with each special needs student. These notes usually come with a file written by a specialist containing a description of the child's condition, suggested strategies for dealing with the condition and an Individual Learning Plan outlining suggested strategies for teaching that individual child. The ILP is a bit like a PD course already written for teachers for that individual child and the good thing about this PD is it is a written plan for teachers to follow with a real live child to apply it to. It is a win-win situation. The child wins by having their work tailored to suit them and the teacher wins by having real-time live professional development. As I have said before, "The best PD a teacher can get is learning how to educate the tricky kids in their class." This includes special needs kids.

So let's have a look at three special needs kids and what they are dealing with.

The ADHD Epidemic

As we have seen throughout this book, Tom was creating great trouble for Miss Young. Unfortunately, Tom is one of the 6.8% of students in our schools who are diagnosed with ADHD, so on average every class of 24 students in Australia will have 1.6 ADHD diagnosed students. Across Australia, according to 2012 figures from Medicare, over 68,000 students in Australia were being medicated for ADHD.

What does this mean for these kids?

Well, for Tom it meant a medication program involving a drug called Ritalin aimed at calming him to a point where he would sit calmly in class and learn like all the other kids. But the Ritalin medication program was having serious side effects with Tom. He was having awful trouble sleeping at night and so he spent night after night tossing and turning into the wee small hours until he would eventually fall into an exhausted sleep. At 7am, Tom was woken in time to catch the bus to school and by the time the school bell rang at 9 o'clock, Tom was usually complaining about feeling tired and being unable to concentrate. It is no wonder. Tom was trying to survive on 3-4 hours sleep a night.

To make matters worse, Tom was not eating well. He suffered from a general lack of appetite and severe stomach cramps which meant he often skipped breakfast and ate two minute noodles for lunch. He suffered from sugar cravings and subsequently drank as much Coke as he could afford. As a consequence Tom's moods alternated between being lethargic and 'woe is me', to hyperactive and aggressive. Tom often ran foul of Miss Young and his fellow classmates which resulted in aggressive outbursts and frequent discussions with the Wellbeing Coordinator.

But how can we expect Tom to learn effectively with all his health issues going on in the background? To be fair, this is not an issue Miss Young has any control over. But it does impact greatly on what she can achieve with Tom in her classroom.

Leading Australian nutritionalist, Dr Michael Sichel, confirms in his book, 'Good News For The Alphabet Kids' that 84% of kids like Tom suffer from bowel dysfunction, 79% experience stomach pains, 74% have very poor sleep patterns and 70% have sugar cravings.

These statistics are backed up by Doctor Murat Pakyurek, an associate clinical professor at the University of California-Davis Medical Center department of psychiatry and the UC Davis M.I.N.D. Institute's ADHD program who says, "for many children, ADHD medications curb restlessness, impulsivity, and inattention well enough for them to flourish at home, school, and on the

playground. But the drugs can also prompt common side effects, such as low appetite, stomach pain, or sleep problems. In rare and serious cases, they can cause heart problems, such as chest pain, liver problems, or even suicidal thoughts."

Dr Pakyurek goes on to suggest the following remedies:

- Decreased appetite: If your child's appetite wanes after taking ADHD medicine, give the dose after breakfast so that he or she will eat better in the morning. Serve a large dinner in the evening, when the drug is beginning to wear off. Keep plenty of healthy snacks on hand.
- Stomach pain or upset: Don't give your child medicine on an empty stomach. For any Gastro Intestinal discomfort, taking the medication with or immediately after food will make a very big difference.
- Sleep problems: Set up a regular bedtime routine that includes relaxing activities, such as bathing or reading. If a stimulant type of ADHD medication prevents your child from sleeping well, ask the doctor about taking the drug earlier in the day or stopping the drug in the afternoon to help your child sleep at bedtime.
- Daytime drowsiness: If the ADHD drug atomoxetine (Strattera) is making your child sleepy during the day, ask about giving the drug at bedtime instead of in the morning. You can also check with the doctor about lowering the dose or dividing the dose and giving it twice a day.
- Rebounding effects: When ADHD drugs wear off in the afternoon or evening, some children have more ADHD symptoms or irritability. To prevent this 'rebounding', ask your child's doctor about using a longer-lasting medication or taking a small dose of fast-acting stimulant later in the day.
- Mood changes: Keep an eye out for changes in your child's mood. If you see changes, such as lessened emotional expression or suicidal thinking, alert your child's doctor right away.
- Heart problems: Since there have been rare reports of serious heart problems in patients taking ADHD drugs, tell your child's doctor about any heart problems in the family.

When the medical profession itself is warning us of such dire health side effects with ADHD medication, it raises the question, "Is it worth putting the physical and mental health of a child at risk just so that they will be calmer at school?" I know school is important, but is it that important to put a child's health at risk?

There is also another risk with ADHD medication that comes from a study supported by the National Institute on Drug Abuse which found that users of Ritalin and similar drugs "showed the highest percentage of cocaine abuse."

The study of 500 students over a period of twenty years found that:

- those who used Ritalin and related drugs had a greater likelihood of using cocaine and other stimulants later in life
- teens who abuse prescription drugs are twelve times likelier to use heroin, fifteen times likelier to use Ecstasy and twenty times likelier to use cocaine, compared to teens who do not use such drugs.

So why is the physical and mental health of thousands upon thousands of kids put at such risk in an attempt keep them quiet enough and subdued enough so that they can sit in our classrooms without disturbing anyone? How is that preparing them for their future? The work of Dr Michael Sichel has consistently proved that the nutritional solution for ADHD is a much better option for the child's short and long term outcomes.

Non-Verbal Learning Disabilities

Dean suffered from Non-Verbal Learning Disabilities and Miss Young had been providing modified activities for Dean on printed worksheets. But she was aghast to read in Dean's Individual Learning Plan, that he had difficulty understanding printed instructions and visual work activities. It said, "Verbal instructions will be vital to help Dean understand written tasks. Tasks must be 'chunked down' into simple small steps and visually presented activities will be difficult for Dean." Miss Young also learnt that Dean's disability affected his ability at spatial relationships, solving problems, making decisions and setting priorities all skills she had been expecting him to use in class.

Miss Young quickly realized that her modified program and worksheets had not suited Dean's learning needs because they were a visual presentation that required the very skills which made learning difficult for Dean.

As she read on she found there were much better ways to help Dean learn:

- provide auditory presentation of his work
- break work down into small, sequential steps
- allow Dean to speak his answers either to a helper or into a voice recorder which could be later checked by an SSO or Miss Young
- utilise his strength at rote learning
- improve Dean's working memory by teaching him verbalising skills and visualization skills
- give Dean some tools to support him with number direction and alignment

Autism Spectrum Disorder

Jack was the third pupil Miss Young had on her special needs list. He was a child with a high functioning autism disorder called Asperger's syndrome so Jack also presented extra challenges for Miss Young. At times he displayed some different behaviours which the other students found rather peculiar and disturbing. Jack was highly sensitive to certain odours, particularly perfume. He struggled to function in a classroom if he detected a perfume that irritated him. When that happened, Jack would simply absent himself from the classroom and go to the library. There were other different behaviours as well. Some days Jack was obsessed with door knobs, other days with people's hair and other days with trees so most kids kept their distance in case they were seen as being friends with a 'weirdo'.

Jack's quirky behaviour marginalized him from many of his fellow students as well as Miss Young and most of his other teachers. Miss Young had even complained to Jack's parents that she couldn't be expected to cater for all Jack's little quirks when she had a classroom of other students to worry about.

But Jack's parents insisted he was entitled to an education just like all the other students in the class so thankfully Miss Young decided to investigate how to accommodate Jack and his learning needs. The first thing she did was to listen to a Dynamic Teacher Talk interview with a lady by the name of Randa Habelrih.

Randa had reared a son with autism and knew all too well the obstacles and issues students with autism face in schools. Her compelling interview convinced Miss Young that she had to do something to help Jack not only learn in class but become an accepted and valued member of the class.

So a new journey of discovery commenced. Firstly, Miss Young read the comprehensive student notes on Jack which helped her to understand Jack's world. She found out what interested Jack, what he enjoyed doing, what his communication challenges were and why he behaved like he did.

But more importantly she learnt some strategies to use with Jack:

- break down Jack's lesson into a set structure of step by step clear instructions
- relate new concepts to Jack to known concepts by linking 'a known' to an 'unknown'
- keeping Jack busy on short activities using high interest topics
- break the session up with reward activities. For example, when Jack has completed a task he is rewarded with 5 minutes free time to play a game on his ipad
- how to use a Time Out Card when Jack was having a difficult moment
- to use praise, humour and laughter to help Jack get through lessons in a positive state of mind
- to position Jack in the seating plan to cater for him feeling comfortable and his lack of awareness of body space
- how to help Jack become well organised at bringing the correct books and utensils to class
- how to help the rest of the class to understand and accept Jack

The next thing Miss Young did was to visit several of Jacks classes during her free periods. This allowed Miss Young to quietly observe Jack at work and to watch how other teachers managed his learning and behaviour. She learnt a lot about Jack just by observing him.

Now Miss Young felt like she had a workable plan to help Jack become an effective and accepted member of the class.

Teachers of alphabet kids require special skills, strategies and attributes.

8 essential attributes for working with special needs kids

1. Developing **rapport** is an important attribute for working with any student but it is critically important for effective work with special needs kids. These kids often have quirky natures and behavioural mannerisms that teachers like Miss Young have to get used to and tolerate. Not every rapport building tool will work with these kids. Often it will take trial and error and a lot of perseverance to see what works and what doesn't work. Finding the key to these kids is the foundation stone for working effectively with them.

2. **Tolerance** is another essential quality for working with special needs kids. These kids have good days and bad days and sometimes things will not go to plan. One of the difficult issues for teachers like Miss Young who is teaching special needs kids in mid to late secondary school is that these students have been subjected to all sorts of remedial classes, testing programs, counseling and modified work over their schooling. Often it gets to a point with them where they are just sick and tired of all the help and the frustration of not keeping up and with people trying to help them.

    A few years ago I ran into a 14 year old called Doug who epitomized these kids. He'd been diagnosed and medicated for ADHD from early in primary school. He'd been through numerous reading catch up classes, counseling, visits to psychologists and by the time I got involved he was highly resistant to help. I managed to develop some degree of rapport with

Doug and designed a completely personalized program built around his interests in motorbikes that had him engaged for a time. But within six months Doug had dropped out of school and that was the last I saw of him. My only advice for teachers of these kids who are highly resistant to help is to search for a way to develop rapport and to try to get them interested in learning again through their interests. There may be times when you need to briefly walk away from these kids as they can be very challenging, difficult and at times aggressive. Sometimes, time to gather your thoughts and composure is essential and skilled teachers recognize when it is time to do that.

3. The ability to find **success** for special needs kids cannot be underestimated. Many special needs students are starved of success and frustrated at seeing their peers learning things they find impossible. A key tool to help these kids is to find ways to give them success so that they can experience themselves learning. It might be counting money, copying Lego models or creating art or craft pieces. It doesn't matter as long as they are interested in the activity and it suits their preferred learning mode. It will help to understand that progress may well be slow and patchy but designing activities where these kids achieve small pieces of success will make a huge difference to their confidence. It will be even better if the 'success' activity can be incorporated into the class activities so that they feel they are learning along with the other students to some extent.

4. The trait of **patience** from teachers will help special needs kids to accept their disability. Once they understand learning may be slower and more difficult for them, special needs kids can accept their disability and learn to work with it instead of against it. This puts them in a much better mindset to make sense of their education and their future. A key goal for working with these kids is to help them find a purpose in life but we need to be patient while they work it out. A valuable tool to help special needs kids accept themselves as they are, is to invite inspirational people/kids from the community to talk to them and/or the class. This will help them identify with themselves and see what other students with disabilities have achieved.

5. The skill of being very well **organised** will support teachers of special needs kids and will make their learning activities so much more powerful. Being organised also helps teachers plan to cater for the 6 basic needs: certainty (routine is essential), uncertainty (the fun factor), significance (feeling of importance through success), connection (belonging to the class), growth (see themselves progressing) and contribution (helping out others). Helping organise special needs kids like Jack to keep all his maths books and equipment in a colour coded plastic pouch will assist him greatly to present to class with the books and resources he will require.

6. The sixth essential attribute is to **'Be Prepared'** for anything. Take notice of this old boy scout motto and be well prepared for special needs kids. Take advice from their ILP (Individual Learning Plan) because it is the best professional development you'll ever do and it will prepare you as to what might work and what might not work with the child concerned. But also be prepared for the unexpected because every day can be different with these kids. Learn to read the signs and go with the flow for a while, but also learn how to redirect attention and make sure your 'coat of many pockets' has some well practised strategies just in case.

7. **Persistence** is a priceless quality for working with special needs students. Some of these kids are going to test teachers every step of the way. What they need to know is that their teacher will be there for them come what may, and even though at times they might walk away, they will be back and they do not give up. Special needs kids also need to know that their teacher is not going to get frustrated with them when learning progress is minimal.

8. The final essential attribute for teachers of special needs students is excellent **communication** skills. Special needs kids often take some understanding when they communicate. Skilled teachers know to always check with the child to ensure they (the teacher) has understood the child's communication and that the child has understood the teacher's communication. Failed communication can break down rapport very quickly. Another vital element of communication is effectively communicating with parents. A

daily written diary or communication book can be a vital resource for efficient messaging on a daily basis between parents and teachers and teachers and parents.

Learning how to teach special needs kids provides teachers with valuable professional learning opportunities to develop skills and strategies that will improve their teaching across the board. These kids will also challenge teachers to further develop the essential attributes required to successfully work with them and to learn how to assist students to develop healthy attitudes about themselves and their place in the world.

Chapter 7 Resources:

1. Recommended Reading:
   - Dealing With Autism (Randa Habelrih)
   - Good News For The Alphabet Kids (Michael Sichel)
   - The Woman Who Changed Her Brain (Barbara Arrowsmith Young)

2. The Arrowsmith Program (www.arrowsmithschool.org)

3. Discussion Paper: 2015 Review of Disability Standards for Education

4. National Institute On Drug Abuse (www.drugabuse.gov)

5. Medicare (https://www.medicare.gov)

6. Dr Murat Pakyuret (http://feelingfit.com/add-adhd/topic/8103-8/story)

7. Dynamic Teacher Talk with Randa Habelrih (www.DynamicTeachingTools.com)

Trapped In Technoeducation

"You don't need to be very good with technology to do very good things with technology."

(Andrew Douch, Evolveducation)

Chapter Eight

Trapped In Technoeducation

The introduction of technology into the classroom has been going on for many years. I guess it commenced way back in the 1960's when television was first introduced into schools along with the computer 'punch cards' we used during our maths classes. Eventually blackboards were replaced by whiteboards, calculators were introduced and interactive projectors we could hook up to computers replaced the old projectors that blew a light bulb every second time we tried to use them.

But the dawdle of technological change in schools became a gallop with the onset of the 21st century. Suddenly schools were encouraged to equip students with personal computers and graphic calculators, overhead projectors were installed to play YouTube videos and DVD movies and by the end of the first decade the Myschool website offered parents unprecedented information about schools and their child's education. As we reach the half way mark of the second decade, the flood of technology options in education has teachers battling to keep their heads above water.

Every child now has access to a computer of some description and most students now have a personal ipad or laptop or netbook they require in class. As well, many students bring iphones and ipods into the classroom. It is not uncommon to see a student listening to music on an ipod, texting on an iphone, and doing schoolwork on an ipad, all at the same time.

Having every child in a classroom with instant access to a learning device as powerful as an ipad is an amazing educational opportunity. However, it causes teachers a lot of grief. As we have seen in Miss Young's class, these devices can become a huge source of distraction for students. The boys in her class played computer games on their ipads at every opportunity and some girls did too which meant Miss Young spent a lot of her time trying to monitor who was doing what on their ipad. There were even times when the ipads were

used for taking photos or videos of classroom incidents that instantly appeared on social media. Cyber bullying was a constant issue bubbling along in the background, disrupting classroom harmony and continually eating up Miss Young's class time as well as that of the Wellbeing coordinator.

School policy in many schools requires that ipads are to be removed from students who use them inappropriately for games, messaging or surfing the web, but this policy has one major drawback. It immediately removes the child's means of accessing his electronic textbooks, his most powerful research tool, his required software programs and his filing system of electronic records. It basically renders him redundant for class activities in some of his classes. So what happens then? Usually it means the child finds himself neutered and unable to function effectively in the classroom which therefore leads to him finding ways of fulfilling his needs for significance and connection in ways which disturb and antagonize other students and teachers alike.

2008 Innovative Australian Teacher of The Year, Andrew Douch, is a leading proponent for using technology in classrooms. He suggests a much more powerful lesson for kids who choose to use their ipads inappropriately is to actually sit down beside them and teach them some ipad etiquette. The underlying message would be that there is a time and place for playing games on the ipad but that time and place is not during class time. These self discipline skills are life skills students can learn as part of the hidden curriculum and are skills which support students for the rest of their lives. These skills could be considered more important than academic skills, so the opportunity to develop ipad etiquette is scuttled if schools adopt authoritarian methods of controlling inappropriate ipad use.

The same can be said for mobile phones which present another challenge for teachers. Students are used to messaging, Facebooking, Twittering and Snapchatting on demand and they find it nigh impossible to ignore these distractions on their phones during class time. In fact you would wonder if kids know who they really are without their mobile phones because they have lived with them in their hands for most of their lives and the phones have become part of the child's identity. The policy in Miss Young's school on the use of mobile phones was tightened up and all phones were to be collected from students at the start of each lesson and returned to students at the end of each lesson. The policy didn't work.

Within a fortnight Miss Young would call for mobile phones to go into the collection basket but no one would own up to having one on them. Mobile phones and their use in the classroom were driven under ground as students devised ingenious ways of hiding their phones and discreetly using them out of Miss Young's view. This silent revolt against the phone policy was almost impossible to police without invading the child's personal privacy and on the odd occasion Miss Young did catch a student using their phone she found that the ensuing discussion fractured rapport and quite often made the issue a personal problem between herself and the student. Confiscating mobile phones completely ignores the wonderful opportunity to teach students appropriate use of mobile phones. As Andrew Douch suggests, why can't we invest time and effort into working with students to help them learn that there is a time and a place and a social etiquette for using mobile phones. It is a very useful life skill which we completely miss out on if phones are routinely confiscated or even banned in our schools.

This opportunity applies with parents too because it is also part of their responsibility to educate their kids about computer and mobile phone use. Andrew Douch makes a great point here when he says, "Before we let somebody on the road, we make sure they are sitting with a responsible adult for 120 hours. But we seem to look at it differently with the internet." And he is correct. Many parents and even teachers simply try to ignore what the kids are doing on these devices. Let's use mobile phones and computers as an opportunity to help kids learn how to be responsible with them in the home and let's sit with kids in class and help them learn to use social media wisely and responsibly and productively.

Guys like Andrew Douch and Michael Carr Gregg provide the following tips for parents to help them manage mobile phone and ipad use in the home:

- parents can set a timed access control on their wi-fi router which shuts down internet access at a predetermined time. For example, a curfew time of say 10pm when internet access shuts down. This removes any temptation a child may have if a friend tries to message them during the middle of the night
- have a charging table where all electronic devices must be on the charging table by 10pm each night
- use parental control features on the devices their child has access to, in order to control which features the child can access

Apart from the management issues ipads and iphones and ipods cause in classrooms, they also offer some wonderful benefits which many teachers utilise. One of the new initiatives at the school Miss Young taught at was an attempt to help teachers take on board any professional learning other staff felt had been beneficial to them. This was an excellent concept which encouraged collaborative learning amongst staff members and offered to help the staff, help each other, to learn new teaching strategies and tools.

Each Wednesday morning at the staff briefing, three staff members would volunteer to make a three to four minute presentation on something new they were using in their classroom. The implementation of modern technology became a dominant theme for the presentations. Week after week presentations on new apps, new software like Google Classroom, Clickview and social media were delivered until even a young gun like Miss Young found it all became a bit of a blur.

It wasn't long before Miss Young felt totally overwhelmed by the sheer volume of educational technology being thrust upon her. It was simply impossible to consider it all. There are over 30,000 educational apps available, software programs for every conceivable maths skill, the Maths Association of Victoria pushing their agenda of technological change in teaching maths and a relentless push from above for teachers to adapt to online reporting, testing programs and parent communication. So Miss Young turned to Andrew Douch for some guidance.

Andrew is an independent education technology consultant with 22 years classroom experience and along the way he has won numerous awards for his work with emerging technologies in education, including:

- the Microsoft Worldwide Innovative Teacher of the Year
- 2007 Australian Government Award for Quality Schooling
- 2008 Microsoft Australian Innovative Teacher of the Year

Andrew's advice to Miss Young was this: It is humanly impossible to take on board all the technology options available to teachers. So when you come across a piece of technology that interests you, try asking yourself these five questions about the item.

Question 1. How does it affect my time? Is it going to require me to put more time in? If so, I'm not interested. But if it is something I can do once and then save my time over and over again, then I'll ask myself the second question. But before I do that, it is also important to consider how it affects my students' time because they are time poor just like teachers. Will it save students time too?

Question 2. Does it do something new or is it just a digitalized way of replicating something we already do? If we are spending all this time and energy to do something we can already do on paper then we should think seriously about whether it is worth it. We should concentrate on tools that do things we can't do the old way.

Question 3. Is it available and free or cheap and can I use it now?

Question 4. Is it something the students like using? Sometimes the best tools just don't resonate with the students so test it first with students to see if they enjoy using it and if they don't, let it go.

Question 5.   Does it demonstrably improve student outcomes? Some tools are really cool but the students aren't learning any better using them. So does the tool solve a problem and improve student outcomes?

If the piece of technology fails to tick all five boxes, then let it pass until another new tool comes along that is worth considering.

One of the issues Miss Young found this overload of technology information was causing, was to distract her from the absolute fundamental element of teaching - the relationship between herself and her students. She came to understand that while modern technology offers some wonderful tools to help engage and inspire and motivate students, it is all pointless if the student - teacher relationship is not working. Andrew's words of advice hit home with Miss Young and suddenly all the new technology she was being exposed to came back into perspective. She decided to take a 'keep it simple' approach to introducing new technology into her classroom and to concentrate her efforts on building relationships with her students.

One of the simple apps Miss Young did choose to trial was called Decide Now. This app was basically a spinning wheel which could be configured for all sorts of uses in the classroom. Miss Young's favourite use for the spinning wheel was where she created a wheel with every class member's name on it. She used this spinning wheel to control class discussions. She would ask a question, spin the wheel and the child whose name was selected was required to answer the question. This simple tool had an amazing affect on class discussions because every child was tuned into the random selection of who the spinning wheel would select to answer the question just in case it was them.

Miss Young also decided to introduce the 'flipped learning' concept that Andrew Douch found so successful. Flipped learning is where teachers create videos and/or podcasts (audio recordings) of their lessons. These videos and podcasts are supported by online discussion groups where students can view or listen to the lessons and then discuss them online. The flipped learning concept has consistently resulted in improved student engagement and a much deeper understanding of the content.

Another equally important benefit of the flipped learning concept is that it frees up class time, one of the most important issues that impacts on teacher creativity, innovation and effectiveness. The old Miss Young always seemed stressed about getting through the curriculum, classroom management and balancing all the outside issues that teachers have to deal with. Now she realised how inefficient some of her habits and practices were so she began to rethink the effectiveness of what she had been doing. She decided to embrace the flipped learning concept wholeheartedly.

Miss Young began creating podcasts and videos of her teaching just as Andrew Douch had suggested. She created separate videos of how to expand $(x + 3)(x - 5)$, how to factorise $x^2 - 8x + 16$ and how to rearrange formulas such as $A = \pi r^2$. She created podcasts of frequently asked questions about Year 9 algebra. She encouraged Josh, Will and Marg to create an online discussion board and before long she found kids like Will, Jake and Kayla joining in with the online discussions. Interest and engagement soared and student performance started to improve. Now Miss Young found time to help Danni and even Tom became more interested in maths.

Miss Young now began looking forward to her Year 9 maths classes and together with all the other strategies she had implemented, her class started to shine. All the old negativity and lack of motivation was replaced by kids who were excited to learn and proud of what they were achieving. Miss Young's calls to parents were replaced by calls from parents asking what she was doing differently. Parents couldn't believe the change in attitude in their kids, they were surprised at the sudden improvement in performance and some parents even enjoyed watching the videos.

Soon, messages started flowing back to Miss Young that kids from other schools were learning from her videos and podcasts.

Education in the 21st century has the opportunity to embrace technology and empower student learning through it. The pace of technological change can be overbearing for teachers but keeping an open and creative mind and a keep it simple approach can empower any teacher to utilise technology to improve student outcomes.

On his website www.evolveducation.com.au Andrew Douch asks us a very interesting question.

"Social networking, the democratization of news and media, instant access to information, instant communication with people, de-specification of work hours and an increasing expectation for work to be meaningful and enjoyable, have changed society more profoundly than many of us realise. But how will these societal changes impact on schools, which still, largely operate in a 20th century, industrial-age model, with a "clock in - clock out" timetable and production-line assessment processes?"

One problem which seems obvious from where I sit in the classroom, is the effect the top down pressure from our politicians and educational movers and shakers is having on our schools and teachers. Their demands to get back to the basics through prescriptive school timetabling and prescriptive National Curriculum, are taking education in this country in entirely the wrong direction. Their hell-bent fascination with PISA rankings and NAPLAN results is alienating thousands of students who drop out of education every year and hundreds of thousands of students still at school who are disengaged and disinterested in what and how we teach.

As Andrew Douch's question suggests, education in this country has not moved with the changes in modern day society and consequently we struggle at preparing our students for the workforce and life in the 21st century. Surely we can do better than having over 40% of our adult population functionally illiterate and innumerate. (abs.gov.au) In the following chapter we will see just what is possible when innovative teachers and leaders think 'outside the box' and inspire student learning.

Modern technology offers some powerful solutions to the educational issues we face and as Andrew Douch shows us, we do not need "to promote high-tech skills in teachers, but rather to encourage widespread adoption of easy-to-use technologies that are high-concept and have the power to transform classroom interaction."

The flipped learning concept is only one of the solutions available to us.

Why can't we provide online classrooms for students who have dropped out of mainstream education? Why can't we give these kids the opportunity to reconnect with education using a format away from the traditional school model? The Khan Academy already offers this style of learning so why can't we align what it offers with our academic standards and requirements?

The School Of The Air has successfully educated isolated kids via radio since 1956. Modern technology offers us the opportunity to give that same choice to all sorts of students from all sorts of situations:

- the school dropout kids
- kids who are sick for prolonged periods or recovering from long term surgery or injury
- kids who are on holidays with parents and need to keep up with their education
- kids who just don't understand what their teacher has taught them and who need a bit of extra work on a specific topic
- kids from dysfunctional homes who can't face going to regular schools
- kids with autism who also find schools unwelcoming
- kids who learn differently than most
- VCE kids who are timetable blocked from the subjects they select (and sometimes need as a prerequisite) could simply access the subject through an online classroom

Digitalising the classroom is only one solution modern technology offers us.

How about we consider these concepts:

- How good would it be for every student in every school to be able to access Barbara Arrowsmith Young's cognitive weakness testing and remedial activity program? Strengthening weak learning areas early in a child's education helps open new learning pathways for them which in turn supports them be the very best they can be.
- How good would it be if 'talk to text' software capable of being programmed to an individual's speech was available for students with cerebral palsy who find written assignments so time consuming and laborious? Is that possible in the 21st century? The short answer is yes, so what is stopping us facilitating the educational assessment requirements for these kids through programmed talk to text facilities?
- How good would it be if kids themselves were encouraged to help educate other kids through filming their own learning activities and putting them on platforms like YouTube? It is called collaborative learning and kids are great at educating other kids. And do you think that this might help meet that child's need for significance, connection and growth?
- How good would it be if modern technology allowed kids to connect their learning with a classroom in Canada or England or South Africa? Is that technologically possible? Of course it is, so what is stopping us from real learning with real students in another country?
- How good would it be if all the homeschooling parents could connect their kids with other homeschooled kids online?
- How good would it be if students were encouraged to use the ipad as a creative and innovative tool to express themselves and to enhance their learning instead of merely using it as a digital library for their text books and a digital way of recording their work using writing software, spreadsheets and presentation programs?

All of these concepts are technologically possible right now so what is stopping us?

One obstacle is our mindset which is stuck in an outmoded school model from 30 to 40 years ago. The old information exchange model we all grew up is fast becoming redundant. Students have access to all the knowledge they need at their fingertips. If they want to know when and where King Henry VI lived, they can have that information within seconds. Kids no longer need to memorise that type of information.

Teaching and teacher training will also need to change. Will forming relationships and rapport still be important? Absolutely, and probably more so than ever before. Teachers must learn how to construct their learning activities in a relevant way for their students. They must be allowed and encouraged to be innovative and creative in the way they approach their teaching. However, as Andrew Douch puts it, "it's not that we need to change everything we do, but we now have a smorgasbord of choices unavailable to teachers even ten years ago. Thinking strategically about how to leverage some of these choices can make us more effective whilst also saving time. It's about teaching smarter, not harder!"

Chapter 8 Resources:

1. Dynamic Teacher Talk: Andrew Douch Interview

2. Andrew Douch www.evolveducation.com.au

3. www.michaelcarr-gregg.com.au

4. www.abs.gov.au

Chapter Nine

What Successful Education Really Looks Like

"*I believe academic achievement is not the most significant indicator of future success. I have said this many times: it is about developing character, working hard to learn, making mistakes and being prepared to learn from them.*"

(Rita O'Brien, Principal Mypolonga Primary School)

What Successful Education Really Looks Like

Over the course of this book so far, we have investigated some fundamental issues affecting the educational outcomes of students. We have looked at issues putting pressure on our teachers, we have looked at issues students bring from home and we've followed how Miss Young reinvented what she was doing with her Year 9 maths class. Poor Miss Young has been through more coaching, training and professional development programs than any one person could possibly cope with. Along the way Miss Young has discovered skills and strategies and tools to completely reinvent the way she operates as a teacher. But now it's time to give Miss Young a rest and to investigate how successful education looks in the real world.

In the real world of education we see success in action every day and yet we often lose sight of it amongst all the negativity and busyness that intrudes in a teacher's work. Every teacher will have some measure of success with their students just like every teacher will have some measure of failure. But some teachers stand out from the pack. Some teachers have a knack for consistent success and so we are going to investigate the common elements that all successful teachers possess.

Last year I was surprised to spot a familiar face at school one day. Familiar is probably not the correct word to use here. It was a face that I recognized but had not seen for probably 40 years. This was a face I knew from my old high school days and here he was filling in as an emergency teacher for the day. As luck had it, on that very day, I ended up working with several students in one of the classes Mr Hunt was covering and it just happened to be a Year 9 maths class.

As quite often happens with emergency teachers, a tricky student we'll call Jedd, decided to test the water with Mr Hunt and not just refuse to work, but to give him some lip. Jedd became argumentative and loud as the rest of the class

watched on. But Jedd was fighting above his weight category. Jedd wasn't to know that Mr Hunt was a master teacher with a 'coat of many pockets' and a toolbelt chock full of tools and strategies complete with a steely determination to succeed. Over the course of that lesson, Mr Hunt turned Jedd from a sullen, disrespectful work refuser, into a friendly face who chose to participate in the some of the class activities.

I remember driving home that night and thinking to myself how lucky I had been to see such a true professional in action. It would have been quite easy for Mr Hunt to have just gone through the motions, taken the lip from Jedd and the money for the day and moved on. But here was a true **educator**, a teacher with the integrity and character and passion and determination to make the effort to make a difference with a difficult student.

Since that day, I have had the privilege to work in class with Mr Hunt on a regular basis. He now teaches full time again after being retired for eight years and the impact he has on his students is remarkable. Mr Hunt epitomizes successful teaching. Does he get it right all the time? No. But he does get consistent success from his students and they love him for it.

So what is it that makes Mr Hunt an outstanding teacher? What is it that makes other teachers consistently successful while some teachers drown in negativity and leave the profession?

Outstanding teachers possess the five key habits of all successful teachers.

The Five Key Habits Of Successful Teachers

Key Habit # 1. They work very hard at building great relationships

Great teachers are very good at building relationships with their students and they understand how and why the rapport they develop with their students is the very foundation of teaching success. Different teachers will use their own unique style of developing rapport with students. Mr Hunt is a master at using repartee to build relationships with his classes. He brings an air of excitement and vitality to his classroom learning environment and engages his students in the learning process.

I'd now like to introduce you to a selection of teachers who have been recognized as the best teachers in the business through the 2014 National Teacher Excellence Awards.

Let us listen to what they say about this first key habit of successful teachers:

- "One thing good teachers have in common is an innate understanding of teaching and a great rapport with students." (Deb Derrick, secondary teacher, QLD)
- "The relationship a teacher has with every child in their class is absolutely vital." (Judy Scotney, primary teacher, QLD)
- "Build strong and valued relationships first and maintain their robustness." (Evangelos Polymeneas, secondary teacher, SA)
- "Teaching is all about relationships. It is so very important that from the first moment that you step into the classroom, you take the time to get to know your students. It is essential that we know their lives, we know their circumstance, and we know their learning preferences. It is so important that throughout the year we can call on that connection that we have with students to help them learn, to bring their lives into the classroom, and to connect their prior knowledge to whatever it is that we are learning in class." (Alyce Cleary, secondary teacher, VIC)
- "Build amazing relationships with your students. If you don't provide them with respect, you can't expect respect back." (Cathryn Ricketts, secondary teacher, NSW)
- "Start with building relationships and everything else will flow." (Ariel Wadick, kinder teacher, VIC)

Building quality relationships is the absolute foundation of successful teaching. If you want to see how Miss Young learned how to develop rapport and relationships with her students, go back to Chapter 4.

Key Habit # 2. They are masters at classroom management

Great teachers are great at managing their classroom. They are so good at it, that it comes as second nature to them and you hardly know they are doing it. They are so skilled at it they nip many problems in the bud before they become issues that affect the learning environment. They also have a great mindset towards working with kids.

I don't know how many times Mr Hunt has quietly said to me through gritted teeth, "I'll win that kid over if it's the last thing I do. I refuse to let him beat me and while he might win this battle, I will win the war!" That is the mindset of a master at classroom management and he wins them over in a way where the child understands that he is better than what he is giving. Being able to have that impact on student mindset is a feature of Mr Hunt's teaching.

Now let's listen to our Master Class of 2014 National Teacher Excellence Award winners as they offer advice to beginning teachers about the importance of effective classroom management:

- "One of the big ones is classroom management. It needs to be part of your personality. I would compare beginning teaching years as the same as learning to drive. It's not until you get your Ps and you are out there by yourself that you really get to learn how to be a driver. It's the same in the classroom." (Tiffany Sirisisavath, primary teacher, NSW)
- "Be firm but fair and always be consistent. Plan, plan, plan. Watch teachers teach. Don't be afraid to ask questions. Most of all, enjoy your job." (Deb Derrick)
- "It is easy to set standards for classroom management too low in the early stages of one's career and nearly impossible to raise them later." (Judy Scotney)
- "Make your goals and expectations clear and stick to it. Don't take the negative personally and remember you're the adult and you're in control and students need to have that." (Evangelos Polymeneas)

Miss Young also showed us how to develop classroom management skills back in Chapter 4.

Key Habit # 3.   They insist on high standards

Great teachers have high expectations of students and they match them by having high expectations for themselves. They see kids as inherently competent with an inbuilt desire to learn and they insist students apply themselves to be the best they can possibly be. Mr Hunt makes his expectations very clear right throughout his teaching lessons. He has high behavioural expectations, high work ethic standards and high learning standards. If his students do not get 80% or more of their work correct, they are expected to go back and practice the exercise some more until they can achieve 80% competency.

All great teachers insist on high standards and that includes our Master Class from the 2014 National Teacher Excellence Awards. Let's listen to what they have to say:

- "It is my goal to try and maintain best practice for all my students. I believe it is my duty to maintain that best practice." (Alyce Cleary)
- "Have a strong image of the child. A child that is competent, creative and curious with an innate desire to learn. Approach each day with pleasure, and laugh often." (David Gilkes, primary teacher, TAS)
- "Senior executives should encourage and support staff to achieve Lead Teacher outcomes and expectations." (Cathryn Ricketts)
- "A student with a great teacher can achieve in half a year what a student with a poor teacher can achieve in a full year." (Judy Scotney)

Noted US educator Rita Pierson says, "Every child deserves a champion, an adult who will not give up on them, who understands the power of connection and insists they become the best that they can possibly be." (Rita Pierson)

And as Tony Robbins reminds us, "What we can or cannot do, what we consider possible or impossible, is rarely a function of our true capability. It is more likely a function of our beliefs about who we are."

Key Habit # 4. They accommodate kids' differences

All great teachers understand that every child is an individual and is different to every other child. They understand how kids learn, they understand that their learning often comes in spits and spurts, they understand that they are all different in numerous ways and they understand that kids will have their ups and downs that will affect their learning progress. Great teachers know that 'one size does not fit all' and that they must accommodate for individual differences even if it means accommodating for differing learning styles between the sexes in this over politically correct world. Great teachers have a profound interest in kids' lives, their goals, their dreams and their expectations. Great teachers facilitate kids' learning, they challenge it, they inspire it and they encourage it.

Great teachers are thought highly of by their students. Some teachers think that their job is to turn up to class, teach the lesson and then move on to their next lesson oblivious to how well the last lesson has gone and how well the students have learnt it. These teachers will argue that it doesn't matter what the kids think of you, it's your job to teach the lesson and their job to learn it. But as Rita Pierson points out, "Kids don't learn from people they don't like." Great teachers are liked because they tick a lot of boxes for their students. They accommodate their needs and differences, they respect the individual child and they never give up on them. Mr Hunt does all that in spades. His students perform well above average and they think highly of him for it.

So let's ask our Master Class what they think are the vital aspects of how great teachers accommodate for student differences:

- "Making sure that you know each child enough to know what their learning needs are, is a challenge." (Brianna Loves)
- "I find it extremely challenging to find ways to encourage that spark, that potential in a student. How can they perform at their best when their basic needs are not being met?" (Tiffany Sirisisavath)
- "I would really like to see genuine differentiation provided for all students." (Denise Ansingh)

- "Support students as much as they 'need' not as much as they 'want'." (Evangelos Polymeneas)
- "Focus on 'listening' rather than 'telling', on 'process' rather than 'product'." (David Gilkes)

We showed Miss Young a lot about understanding how kids learn and how to accommodate their differences back in Chapter 2.

Key Habit # 5. Passion for making a difference

Master teachers are universally passionate about their job and how they can make a difference in a child's life. As we have already seen, Mr Hunt was so passionate about making a difference he took on Jedd when he was emergency teaching. But his passion shines through in lots of other ways too:

- His passion for knowing each child thoroughly means that when parent-teacher interviews come along, he can articulate to parents exactly where their child is functioning, how they are performing in an academic sense and how well they are applying themselves.

- His passion makes him determined to improve and incorporate new and creative resources and strategies into his teaching even though he has been in education for over 40 years.

- His passion for seeing kids take flight and aim high is seen every day when he challenges students to extend their learning using accelerated learning programs.

- His passion for supporting the 'strugglers' and accommodating the different learning needs of students means these kids know they are important in Mr Hunt's eyes.

- His passion for the job means Mr Hunt fronts up every day and despite all the incomprehensible policy changes, bureaucratic red tape, overwhelming documentation and political correctness that invades teachers' lives, he turns up and teaches well anyway.

And do you know why?

Here is a little story to show you one reason why Mr Hunt does what he does with so much passion.

We have already seen that Mr Hunt uses repartee to great effect with his students. Just recently, he walked into his Year 11 Physics class and said, "for a bit of fun I had a grizzle that my birthday is always during the school holidays and so I always miss out on a staff birthday morning tea. The students made a bit of fun of me and it was great but next lesson they presented me with this 21st birthday card."

This is what the card said:

> "Dear the 'Wiz'
>
> We may have had our maximums and minimums but our respect for you is exponential.
>
> You always seem to radiate energy into our education even if you sometimes go on a tangent.
>
> But that is just a sine that you love teaching us.
>
> From the original physics crew

As Mr Hunt told me his story and showed me his card, he said, "That's the sort of thing that makes this all worthwhile. That's why I do what I do." At that moment, all I could do was to nod in agreement. The lump in my throat prevented me from saying anything.

This book is all about empowering teachers to feel good about their work despite all the 'noise' going on around them. And dotted all over our country are wonderful examples of teachers and schools who have achieved outstanding success despite the dysfunctional teaching environment many teachers find themselves in. We can learn from these teachers and schools and use them as beacons of light to model our own approach to our work in the class room and at school.

In the previous chapter we came across the outstanding work of Andrew Douch. Here is a teacher who has been recognized as an outstanding and innovative teacher and I'm sure Andrew appreciates this list of awards:

2007 Australian Government Award for Quality Schooling
2007 Microsoft Victorian Innovative Teacher of the Year
2008 Microsoft Australian Innovative Teacher of the Year
2008 Microsoft Worldwide Innovative Teacher of the Year
2008 Victorian Education Excellence Award for Curriculum Innovation
2010 IMS Australian Learning Impact Award (third place)
2011 IMS Global Leadership Award
2011 Australian College of Educators. World Teachers' Day Award.

But Andrew's real success comes from his work at making a difference in the lives of his students. His flipped learning classroom not only raised his students' grades by an average of two levels, he got them excited about what they were learning at school and it wasn't just to help them pass their exams. Andrew inspired his students to become life long learners.

Let's listen to one of his former students when it was suggested she was no longer a biology student because she had finished her exams.

She replied, "I'm a true student. I'm enrolled in life. I don't just learn because of the assessment ahead of me. I learn because I love learning. So when the assessment is over, I still see myself as a student. In Biology I learned more than just proteins and DNA. I learned what it means to be connected with educated people who love learning and there is no reason why that should be over just because I've completed the exam. Assessments should measure learning, not be the reason for it. I want to keep learning Biology so I still consider myself a Biology student, so don't say I'm not!"

That is what outstanding teachers like Andrew Douch do. They inspire kids to be life long learners, they build character in their students and they exhibit the five key habits of successful teachers:

- Andrew was brilliant at building relationships and rapport not just in the classroom, but using social media.
- He was a master at classroom management because he had the kids so highly engaged and excited to be in class.
- Andrew achieved very high standards using the flipped classroom concept. In fact, he raised student grades by an average of two levels!
- He accommodated kids differences by creating podcasts and video tutorials and hands-on learning activities. He gave every child a way to participate fully in his learning activities.
- He was absolutely passionate about his work and that piece of student feedback we just looked at proves just how passionate Andrew was.

Andrew Douch is the sort of man I want teaching my grandkids. Andrew Douch is the sort of man who will inspire them, and challenge them, and nurture them when they need it and educate them about life.

So we have looked at successful teaching and what common elements successful teachers possess. Now it is time to turn our attention to successful schools and what makes them special and shine like the brightest star in the sky.

Anyone who knows me will know that I am a long time supporter of the Hawthorn Football Club. During my life the HFC have won every one of the 13 Premierships they have collected so far and that success comes down to one thing. During the time since their first Premiership in 1961, they have had three outstanding, long term coaches that have delivered ten of their thirteen Premierships. Ironically, two of those coaches were teachers.

The inaugural Hawthorn Premiership coach of 1961, John Kennedy, actually gave up his job as Hawthorn coach to take up the role as Principal at Stawell Technical School in 1965. While there he took the Stawell Football Club to three grand finals in a row and although he would never have known it, his three quarter time addresses to the players showed young supporters like me just how valuable inspirational leadership is. John Kennedy, Alan Jeans and Alastair Clarkson have each had long term outstanding success at the Hawthorn Football Club because they taught process, they built character and a sense of community in their teams, they worked incredibly hard and they were visionary enough to change the way their teams played the game of football.

Now I know not everyone is an Australian Football fan like me. So who is it for you? Who is the inspirational leader you can relate to? Maybe it is Sir Alex Ferguson at Manchester United, or Bill Wash at the San Francisco 49ers or Phil Jackson at the Chicago Bulls and the Los Angeles Lakers; all outstanding coaches who taught process and built character. It is exactly the same in education.

The common element for all successful schools is outstanding leadership which focuses on the processes of learning and teaching instead of the NAPLAN results and ATAR scores. Successful leaders understand that if they get the process right, the results in NAPLAN scores and ATAR scores will fall into place.

And that is exactly what has happened at Mypolonga Primary School in South Australia under the visionary leadership of Rita O'Brien. This is the sort of school I want my grandkids to go to. Here is a school where kids get excited about their learning, where the whole community is involved in the kids' education, where strong values and life skills are taught under an astute and supportive leader and her staff. Rita has made this school like a honey pot to bees and has a waiting list of students from all over the district just wanting to be part of this outstanding school community and its rigorous learning programs.

A quick flick through the Mypolonga School & Community Newsletter will give us an insight into what happens at Mypolonga Primary School:

- Firstly they live the **TIGER** values throughout the school: **T**eamwork, **I**ntegrity, **G**enerosity of Spirit, **E**xcellence, **R**espect. These values are incorporated into everything that happens at this school. They even sing about them.
- **Rita's Roar** delivers philosophical ideals, thank you's, explanations about programs and enthusiasm for what the kids are achieving. It oozes with passion. Here are a few snippets:
- "At Mypo, we believe that learning starts at birth and never finishes."
- "The variety of master classes offered this year has been astounding. There is a real 'buzz' about the school as we all learn new things together."
- "Last Wednesday, we recognized the amazing work our SSOs (Student Service Officers- edubabble for teacher aides) do on a day to day basis."
- "I love seeing kids who are passionate. What they are passionate about doesn't matter, as long as there is passion."
- "Well done to everyone involved in Jump Rope For Heart. It's great to see our young kids who were struggling to skip two years ago, showing incredible proficiency."
- The master classes Rita referred to above are a tradition at Mypo' Primary. Each year, students are able to try and enjoy a range of activities provided by staff, parents, **community members** and even students. There were 27 master classes offered this year including everything from string pictures to bush art to Farmer Jones Paddock (a paddock donated to the school which is being turned into a Healthy Eating Garden and a Sensory Playground).
- They run karate classes to teach kids **self defence** and the **self discipline** to avoid conflict.
- They run a vibrant Student Representative Council to develop **leadership** skills and to train students in working to **contribute** to the school community.
- They provide information and **advice to parents**. Information about, 'Why Is Sleep So Important' and 'How To Develop Oral Skills At Home' are just a sample of what is offered.

- There is a special section devoted to positive feedback from visitors off 'The Proud Mary' to the school shop. Yes, the students here have operated a school shop **business** every Friday (including school holidays) since 1996. This shop is open to the public and has regular visits of tourists from 'The Proud Mary' paddle ship. Many items for sale are made by the students and as well they sell local produce and art and craft on consignment. The students rotate through a range of roles in the shop and their assessments in those roles are recorded in each student's Student Shop Assessment Book. Students receive proficiency badges in the skills they learn and they work towards accumulating 25 **excellence** badges which then qualifies them for a **Certificate of Financial Management** and as accredited assessors to mentor and assess other students. The day I visited Mypolonga School Shop, the students and teachers were on holidays but that didn't stop 15 kids and a number of staff from volunteering to don their school uniform and open up the shop.

And Rita and her merry band of students' day didn't end there. That same day, they were also preparing 130 meals for a **community** function later that evening which involved the students preparing and serving at the function. Rita and her team are currently busy writing another set of roles and rotations for this Community Catering Program which operates four times a year so that another set of **practical skills** can be developed into an authentic and rigorous learning program.

Rita O'Brien's school is all about the kids. Everyone is encouraged to take part in the decision making and students from all levels do just that. Students sit in on a variety of meetings throughout the school including:

- staff meetings where students and parents are encouraged to have input
- Student Representative Committee (SRC) meetings. "Students from Reception to Year 7 are elected to the School Representative Council for a two-term tenure. The SRC represents the views of the students of Mypolonga Primary School. It is an integral part of the decision-

making which occurs throughout the school. Responsibilities of members include attending SRC meetings, organising fundraising events for the school and negotiating and implementing changes and improvements within the school." (Mypolonga PS Parents' Handbook)

- the Governing Committee has input from two SRC representatives
- the Sustainability Committee which works on how the school can remain relevant and sustainable to the kids in an ever changing world
- the School Improvement Committee meetings which makes decisions on how the school can be improved and then implements those decisions
- the Shop Finance Committee meetings run by students who monitor the shop finances and approve where the $6,000 plus profits from the shop are allocated each year

At Mypo, these committees are not seen as bodies which control student learning and what happens there. They are seen as bodies which empower students to have a say in what happens at the school. Student leadership and input is highly valued at Mypolonga and has been the seed from which the school shop has grown, the school logo has been developed and the TIGER values have originated. The school focuses on educational processes that will have lasting benefits for the kids and along the way it builds a school community which develops character through real-life programs, community involvement and a visionary Individual Growth Program for every child.

The Individual Growth Program is called the Elly (short for elephant) Program, and it is a goal setting program each student develops with their parents and teachers to develop key competencies in things like resilience, caring and contribution, self belief and all the success mindset and emotional intelligence attributes we looked at in Chapters 5 and 6. The Elly Program develops an Emotional Intelligence Wheel for each student, a visual representation of their growth and development in these key competencies in the hidden curriculum. This program develops young men and women with purpose and resilience and wisdom through practical real-world experience and it underpins the outstanding academic achievements of students at Mypolonga.

This school scores above average NAPLAN results. The school average in most of the disciplines tested through NAPLAN is at least one standard and at times two standards above the required standard:

DECD		Mypolonga Primary School				
Year Level	Standard Expected	Reading	Writing	Spelling	Grammar Punctuation	Numeracy
3	3 or above	5	4	4	5	6
5	5 or above	7	6	6	7	7
7	6 or above	7	6	7	7	7

Mypolonga Primary School epitomizes everything I believe is important in education:

1. Rita and her teaching staff display an outstanding mindset towards their teaching and leadership within their school.

2. There is a deep understanding of the children to meet the needs of certainty, uncertainty, connection, significance, growth and contribution in everything they do. They take a holistic approach to education which includes the Stephanie Alexander Healthy Eating Program and a daily staff and student exercise program.

3. This school incorporates parent input into everything they do including staff meetings.

4. Very high behavioural expectations are met in class and in everything thing they do at Mypolonga.

5. There is considerable effort spent developing a success mindset in the kids. The 'Okay Isn't Excellence' motto underpins this attitude.

6. The Mypolonga community promotes emotional intelligence skills through the Elly program to help students develop the self science they need to thrive in the 21st century.

7. Every effort is made to respect and nurture special needs students and empower them to be the very best they can possibly be.

8. They strategically incorporate technology into the classroom and other school programs.

Myplonga Primary School is an outstanding school led by an outstanding principal. But there are other inspirational principals we could just as easily take a look at if space permitted. Principal Michael Allen at Hamilton Island State School in Queensland has led his school to four state awards over the last twelve months.

John Marsden has led Candlebark School to fly in the face of all that is cherished in most private schools and yet boasts a growing school population of students excited about their learning through an array of practical learning programs. This is a school with a difference. Under John's visionary leadership, students wear work clothes to school so that they can 'get dirty' learning through practical farm based learning programs. Kids eat what they produce at Candlebark and again there is a long waiting list of students eager to learn there.

Then there is Peter Hutton and what he is doing at Templestowe College. Again, this is a school with a difference. "We have deliberately removed many of the restrictions that traditional schools place on students, such as year level structures, single age classes and authoritarian hierarchical structures. We do have a vibrant and productive learning atmosphere, scheduled class times, a uniform which is worn with pride, and very high standards of respect shown for one another." Peter Hutton, Principal, Templestowe College

We need more innovative and inspirational leaders in our schools. Not leaders who lead through their position of power and authority. We need leaders who lead by inspiring us to make a difference in a child's life. We need leaders who lead us not because we have to be led, but because we want to.

Sir Ken Robinson puts it like this, "The real role of leadership in education, and I think it's true at the national level, the state level, at the school level, is not and should not be command and control. The real role of leadership is climate control, creating a climate of possibility. And if you do that, people will rise to it and achieve things that you completely did not anticipate and couldn't have expected."

Outstanding leaders like Rita O'Brien do exactly this. They create a climate of possibility and inspire everyone around them, teachers, parents, the outside community and most importantly, the students. (Even bald headed old authors become inspired by being around Rita.)

School leadership in the 21st century is not an easy job. School leaders are affected by the same issues which affect our teachers plus they shoulder the ultimate responsibility of the school's overall performance and standing in the community. However, our school leaders and every school teacher are in a position to make a difference in a child's life and to reshape education at the very heart of the education process, the relationship between the child and the teacher.

As Rita Pierson said in her TED talk, "Teaching and learning should bring joy. How powerful would our world be if we had kids who were not afraid to take risks, who were not afraid to think and who had a champion? Every child deserves a champion, an adult who will not give up on them, who understands the power of connection and insists they become the best that they can possibly be. Is this job tough? You betcha, oh God, you betcha. But it is not impossible. We can do this. We are educators. We are born to make a difference."

Unfortunately, part of our job to reshape education will be to help our politicians understand what is truly important in education. Unfortunately, they just do not understand. They think the focus of education should be on PISA rankings, ATAR scores, NAPLAN results and truancy levels and they'll use all sorts of threats, intimidation and authoritarian means to try to get what they want. It is just not working.

What we need to show our politicians is that the real success stories in education prove that education works much better when innovation and creativity is encouraged and the focus is on the process of education; instilling great values, building great relationships, concentrating on whole-child development and teaching through community involvement. That's when kids get excited about their learning; that's when they become empowered learners; that's when motivation and purpose soars and that's when the NAPLAN results improve.

I have a dream to make a difference in the way we approach education. There are way too many kids disengaged from their education, there are way too many kids entering the workforce feeling totally unprepared, there are way too many kids leaving school functionally illiterate or innumerate, and there are way too many kids who drop out of school and university for that matter.

I believe we can do far better than what we are doing and I believe it is our teachers who are in the best position to reshape education. But just reading about it or talking about it won't achieve anything! We need action, massive action just like Rita O'Brien has shown us at Mypolonga Primary School.

Today, in fact right now, please make a choice to take action and just DO something. Select a tool to implement, practice a strategy, listen to an expert on a Dynamic Teacher Talk, search for some teacher resources on the Dynamic Teaching Tools website, join the dynamic teaching flock and have your say on teaching and education on the Dynamic Teaching Tools Discussion Board at the www.DynamicTeachingTools.com. Whatever it is, just DO something and while you're at it, give us some feedback on my book. I'd love to hear your thoughts.

Together we can make a difference.

Our grandkids' future depends on it.

Yours in education,

Ian Davies
Aussie Kids Coach
enquiry@aussiekidscoach.com

Chapter 9 Resources:

1. Dynamic Teacher Talk Podcasts at www.DynamicTeachingTools. com from:
   - Trevor Hunt (Secondary School Teacher) This interview reveals the story of a highly successful teacher who continues to evolve his teaching and inspire students after 40 years of classroom teaching.
   - Rita O'Brien (Mypolonga Primary School Principal) This interview showcases how great leaders inspire those around them: teachers, parents, the local community and of course, most importantly, the kids. We'll also hear how Rita has created a culture of success at Mypolonga
   - Andrew Douch (www.evoleducation.com) In this interview Andrew displays as a creative and thoughtful thinker who understands kids and knows how to inspire them through innovative use of technology.

2. Rita Pierson TED Talk, 'Every Kid Needs A Champion'

3. Hamilton Island State School (www.hamiislass.eq.edu.au)

4. Candlebark School (www.candlebark.info)

5. Mypolonga Primary School (http://mypolongaps.sa.edu.au/a/)

6. Templestowe College (www.templestowec.vic.edu.au)

Author Profile

Ian Davies

Author, Educator, Entrepreneur, Tutor, and Life Coach

Ian is an international author, educator, and highly sought-after tutor and life coach.

Although Ian now excels at motivating students, he recalls failing kindergarten and just barely surviving secondary school. One of the things that kept him going at school was his strong interest in sport. In his youth, Ian was an award-winning athlete that excelled in tennis, football, golf, volleyball, badminton, and squash.

Ian's desire to improve the lives of others led him to Ballarat Teachers College. After becoming a qualified primary school teacher, he proudly served as the headmaster of Macorna Primary School and Jung Primary School and then worked in special education at Pleasant Creek Special School for 11 years.

After retiring from teaching, Ian returned to farming having been raised on a dairy and sheep farm and carting sheaf hay for $12 a day when he was 15 years old.

He converted his farm to biodynamic farming principles and worked as a professional wool classer for other local farms for more than 20 years. However, education was never far from Ian's thoughts. During this period he spent 11 years on Concongella School Council, serving 3 of those years as School Council President.

Fortunately for those Ian has helped over the years, he began to tutor his neighbour's kids. After word of his success spread and he realised the satisfaction he felt from helping kids overcome their anxiety about learning,

Ian decided to offer professional tutoring and coaching and launched Aussie Kids Coach in 2008. He has written a number of educational self help books and programs which sell across the world such as:

- Spelling Rules For Kids
- Why Your Kid Can't Read And What You Can Do About It
- Punctuation Rules For Kids
- The Teachers Toolbox series of teaching tools for teachers
- … and so on

Seeking to do the most good wherever he went, Ian shared his talents as a tutor and coach at Halls Gap Primary School, Concongella Primary School, Stawell Secondary School, Marian College, as well as his private clients.

To further improve his skills, Ian completed Cert IV in Life Coaching at the Life Coaching Institute of Australia, as well as Strategic Intervention training and Marriage Education and Divorce Prevention training at the Robbins-Madanes Training Centre. Ian the entrepreneur now operates three related businesses in addition to his farm business: Aussie Kids Coach, Aussie Business Tools, and Your Aussie Life Coach.

Ian is a life member of the Stawell Athletic Club where he is the Corporate Marquee Coordinator and a member of the Finance Sub-Committee. He takes pride in having never missed seeing a Stawell Gift Final live. Ian is also a member of Legacy Australia through the Ararat Legacy Club, and he is a member of the Biodynamic Agriculture Association of Australia.

Ian is also an avid traveler, having visited New Zealand multiple times as well as the west coast of Canada and the west coast of the United States.

Ian Davies is the author of "Dynamic Teaching In The 21st Century… Empowering Tools And Strategies For Teachers Who Want To Make A Difference" and lives in country Victoria with his wife Robyn, his three children and his grandchildren.

Resources

Dynamic Teacher Tools website

www.DynamicTeachingTools.com

Why the website?

I believe those of us who work at the grassroots level of education can reshape education from the ground up.

I believe teachers are in the best spot to make the biggest impact on student learning and student wellbeing.

The Dynamic Teaching Tools website is an important plank in my quest to make a difference in the lives of as many schoolkids as possible.

How the Dynamic Teacher Tools website works:

There are many, many free teacher resources and learning tools on the website.

For a small yearly membership fee, (actually less than $1 a week for parents and teachers) teachers and parents and schools can access my complete tool chest of educational resources. I hold nothing back in the way of teaching resources from my loyal members.

What you get access to:

- hundreds upon hundreds of free teacher resources
- pre tested printable teacher resources and worksheets
- ready to use school projects
- hundreds of charts, maps and posters designed to liven up any classroom and support student learning
- wellbeing programs for every level of student
- … and lots, lots more!

ASIC MoneySmart
Teaching Program for Schools

Ian thoroughly recommends and supports the MoneySmart Teaching program.

Helping schools get MoneySmart

Knowing how to manage money and make confident and informed financial decisions are core life skills.

ASIC's MoneySmart Schools Program recognises and supports Australian schools that help their students develop good money habits. The program also promotes the importance of consumer and financial literacy to families and their local community.

Dynamic Teacher Talks: Series 1

A set of six teacher enhancement talks designed to assist you in enhancing your teaching by giving you first hand access to expert opinion on a whole range of educational topics. We want you to find new pathways to teaching success and fulfilment and the Dynamic Teacher Talks are designed to do just that.

Learn from the experts:

Talk 1: Andrew Douch (www.evoleducation.com) In this interview Andrew displays as a creative and thoughtful thinker who understands kids and knows how to inspire them through innovative use of technology.

Talk 2: Randa Habilreh, author of 'Dealing With Autism. How I successfully raised my child with autism and how you can too.'

Talk 3: Trevor Hunt (Secondary School Teacher) reveals the story of a highly successful teacher who continues to evolve his teaching and inspire students after 40 years of classroom teaching.

Talk 4: Rita O'Brien (Mypolonga Primary School Principal) showcases how great leaders inspire those around them: teachers, parents, the local community and of course, most importantly, the kids. You'll hear how Rita has created a culture of success at Mypolonga and a series of authentic educational programs which have her students kicking goals in school and in their community

Talk 5: Pete Burdon author of 'Media Training For Modern Leaders' and an expert in helping schools develop crisis management plans.

Talk 6: Terry Phillips, a parent who opens his heart about his own education and his worst fears for his child's education. Listen to Terry's frank and heartbreaking story of watching his son fail at school and learn what Terry did about it.

Arrowsmith
School

Strengthening Learning Capacities

Ian Davies endorses the Arrowsmith Program for changing the lives of students struggling with learning disabilities

At Arrowsmith, we specialize in strengthening learning capacities rather than simply learning ways to compensate for learning disabilities. We have been helping children, youth, and adults with learning disabilities to overcome their challenges and achieve academic success since 1978.

The Arrowsmith Program is based on the application of sound neuroscientific research for over 35 years, demonstrating that it is possible to help students strengthen the weak cognitive capacities underlying their learning disability.

Our goal is to help students become effective, confident, and self-directed learners. Our program is offered at schools throughout North America, Australia, New Zealand and Asia.

www.arrowsmithschool.org

Dynamic Teaching Tools
Workshops And Presentations

Workshops Including:

- Leadership Workshop For Kids

- Leadership For School Leaders

- The Art of Self Science Teacher Development Program

- The ROAR learning system in action

- … and more. We are constantly developing different workshops to specific requests from schools. Let us know and we can design a workshop for your needs

Presentations Including:

- 10 Quick And Easy Short Cuts For Ruining The Education Of Any School Child

- How The English Language Really Works

- Teaching practices and strategies to support individual needs of students

- The Top Ten Fears Kids Bring To The Classroom

- … and more. We are constantly developing different presentations to specific requests from schools. Let us know and we can design a presentation for your needs

Go to www.DynamicTeachingTools.com for full details of the workshops and presentations offered by Ian Davies and his team at Aussie Kids Coach.

wisa Wellbeing in Schools Australia

A national, 'not for profit' organisation established in 2015 and endorsed by Ian Davies

Vision

School communities building resilience in all students, especially the most marginalised and those at risk of marginalisation, so they can reach their potential in education and in life.

Purpose

To work collaboratively with school communities in building a strategic whole of school approach to health and wellbeing that creates a socially just environment where all students can thrive, particularly those at risk of or who are being marginalised.

WISA offerings:

- **Building capacity of Leaders of Wellbeing/Wellbeing Coordinators**
  - One day 'Essential basic training'
  - One day 'Consolidating Essentials'
  - One day 'Advanced training for Wellbeing Leaders'

- **Whole school staff training**
  - Strategies for supporting your most vulnerable students

- **Wellbeing training for school leaders (principals and governance)**
  - Embedding Wellbeing in your school community

- **School Wellbeing Network membership (Commencing January 2016)**
  - Mentoring support
  - Wellbeing network meetings
  - School Wellbeing Member Blogs
  - School Wellbeing Newsletter

Jac Van Velsen 0423 823 145   **Ros Pretlove 0437 758 463**
www.wisawellbeing.com.au   ABN: 61 605 477 987